Chinese American Family Therapy

Marshall Jung

Chinese American Family Therapy

A New Model for Clinicians

Jossey-Bass Publishers • San Francisco

Jossey-Bass books and products are available through most bookstores. To contact Jossey-Bass directly, call (888) 378-2537, fax to (800) 605-2665, or visit our website at www.josseybass.com.

Substantial discounts on bulk quantities of Jossey-Bass books are available to corporations, professional associations, and other organizations. For details and discount information, contact the special sales department at Jossey-Bass.

For sales outside the United States, please contact your local Simon & Schuster International Office.

 Manufactured in the United States of America on Lyons Falls Turin Book. This paper is acid-free and 100 percent totally chlorine-free.

Library of Congress Cataloging-in-Publication Data

Jung, Marshall.
    Chinese American family therapy : a new model for clinicians / Marshall Jung.
      p. cm.
    Includes bibliographical references and index.
    ISBN 0-7879-4045-3
    1. Chinese Americans—Mental health.   2. Family psychotherapy.
I. Title.
RC451.5.C45J86   1998
616.89'156'089951073—dc21   97-51420
                                             CIP

FIRST EDITION
HB Printing   10 9 8 7 6 5 4 3 2 1

Contents

List of Tables and Figures

Tables

Figures

List of Appendixes

This book is dedicated to
Richard, Judy, Brittany, Eileen, and David.

Acknowledgments

Many people supported me in the writing of this book. I am especially indebted to Alan Rinzler and Judith Hawkins for their editorial support. Both read my manuscript, made editorial suggestions, and helped me to conceptualize important ideas.

I owe a special thanks to the many people who took time away from their busy schedules to provide me with important information for my final chapter. These include Gene Chen, Stephen Cheung, Larry Dodson, Ron Florendo, Herbert K. Hatanaka, Rudy Kao, Margaret Y. Law, Tri Huu Le, Gladys Lee, Stephanie Lee, Lawrence J. Lue, Theresa H. Liu, David Luk, Beckie Masaki, Glenn L. Masuda, Yoshi Matusushima, Dennis Murata, Phuoc (Frank) Nguyen, Alan Y. Oda, Alan Shinn, Gloria Tan, Yumi Verdi, Amy Watanabe, Mike Watanabe, Steven Wong, Joyce W. Yeh, Gladys Yoou, and Helen Yu. I am also thankful for the moral support given to me by my colleagues Lucy Cardona and Ira Neighbors.

Finally, I would like to thank *Asian Week* magazine, publisher of *Asians in America: 1990 Census* and Bill O. Hing and Ronald Lee, editors of *Reframing the Immigration Debate,* for allowing me to use data from their books. Their generosity saved me numerous hours in doing research to obtain the data I needed.

M.J.

Chinese American Family Therapy

Introduction

Chinese American Family Therapy (CAFT) is a complex, comprehensive, and pragmatic model of therapy designed to help Chinese American families. Since the Immigration and Nationality Act of 1965, the number of Chinese immigrating to this country has increased at an unprecedented rate. By the turn of the century it is expected that the Chinese in the United States will number well over two million. Many of the newly arriving immigrants, as well as U.S.-born Chinese, are in need of mental health, child welfare, and social services. This book was written to provide both Chinese and non-Chinese therapists with a culturally sensitive therapeutic model to assist these individuals and families.

CAFT is based upon my life experience, professional training, and clinical practice with both Chinese and non-Chinese clients. It is an eclectic model, combining crisis intervention, case management, general systems theory, and social learning theory with family integration theory, a new paradigm for understanding the intrapersonal and interpersonal dynamics of Chinese families. CAFT can be used in conjunction with other clinical models such as Solution Focused Therapy, Structural Family Therapy, and Strategic Therapy. The model's eclecticism allows it to be used in all the settings in which counseling services are provided—mental health clinics, child welfare agencies, and residential treatment programs, to name a few. It also allows therapists to build upon and add a dimension to what they already know.

Dispelling the Myths

That there are clear differences between Chinese and Western culture is a fact; however, in addition to introducing a new model of practice, a second purpose of this book is to dispel myths held by many American mental health professionals regarding Chinese Americans. One such myth holds that the Chinese are a model minority, are all successful, and take care of the needs of their own. In fact, 8 percent of native-born Chinese and 16 percent of immigrants live in poverty; most of these people receive public assistance. Another myth is the belief that all Chinese are honorable and kind, put the needs of their family before their own, and respect their elders. Although it is true that Chinese are family-centered, they are like any other group and display the full range of human attitudes and behaviors. Some are sensitive, responsible, sacrificing, and just, but others are narcissistic, drug-dependent, abusive, disrespectful, and unfair.

Another myth is that all Asian Americans are alike, when in fact each ethnic group is distinct, with its own history, religious and philosophical beliefs, language, art, customs, traditions, and so on. Many people also believe in the myth that the Chinese are a homogenous ethnic group, when really they consist of several distinct ethnic groups. In addition, Chinese also differ based on their country of origin; many Chinese come to the United States from Taiwan, Hong Kong, or Vietnam. It is therefore very important that clinicians be aware of the major cross-cultural issues between Asian groups and between various Chinese groups.

Finally, many mental health professionals believe the myth that Chinese do not use psychological services. It is true that Chinese are reluctant to seek professional assistance for problems related to mental illness or interpersonal problems. This is a result of their views on mental illness and the personal shame associated with using help outside the family. However, experience and research have shown that Chinese will use psychological services when (1) they have been informed of their availability, (2) they are provided with easy access to them, (3) the delivery system is culturally sensitive, and (4) the professional staff is competent.

A third purpose of this book is to dispel the myths Asian mental health professionals have toward treatment of Chinese clients. One myth is that you only need to be bilingual and bicultural to provide effective treatment. This, of course, is not true. In my training of Asian American professionals, I have observed insensitive and incompetent bilingual and bicultural therapists who alienated, rather than helped, their clients. I believe that what is even more important than language capacity and cultural affinity is competency and the ability to provide a safe and supportive atmosphere in which clients can be helped to grow and change.

Another myth is the view that because Chinese culture is shame-based, Chinese are more sensitive to shame than non-Chinese clients, and therefore we need to create a treatment atmosphere in which they do not "lose face." There is no empirical evidence to substantiate this belief. No one wishes to be embarrassed or made to feel ashamed. A guiding principle for any therapist is to treat all clients, Chinese or otherwise, with respect, sensitivity, and understanding, and to ensure that their dignity is never threatened or challenged.

Another myth is that Chinese are motivated only by their cognitive processes and that affective interventions are inappropriate. This implies that Chinese are not influenced by their emotions or capable of expressing their feelings, neither of which is true. This myth also stereotypes Chinese as being one-dimensional and emotionally limited. Although Chinese may not verbally express their feelings, this does not mean that they are not influenced by them. In working with Chinese clients, therapists should feel free to use the full range of interventions at their disposal, including the use of affect. The basis for any intervention, however, should be predicated on the unique needs, personality, and psychological profile of each client.

Finally, there is the myth that non-Chinese therapists cannot be effective in working with traditional Chinese families. If this were true, it would imply that to be effective in treatment, the ethnicity of therapists and their clients would always need to match. This, of course, is absurd. Instead, what is important is that therapists be sensitive to and aware of their clients' cultural backgrounds. A major objective of this book is to assist therapists in this area by helping them to understand Chinese culture and cross-cultural issues, so that they may be more effective in helping their Chinese clients.

Overview of the Book

The major theoretical concepts and principles of practice in CAFT are based in Chinese, rather than Western, culture. They are presented in a manner that is easily learned and applied. Case examples are given to demonstrate their application to various circumstances, family constellations, and presenting problems.

CAFT represents a synthesis between my personal growth as a first-generation Chinese American and my professional growth as a therapist. Chapter One describes the story of that synthesis. The script recounts how my family, like the families of so many other Chinese immigrants, addressed the issues of assimilation into American society and the problems they had to face and overcome. It describes how I, like others of my generation, had to struggle, experience emotional pain, and learn to integrate American and Chinese culture. Finally, the script describes my evolution from a structural family therapist to a practitioner who can select from a variety of methods and models to meet the unique needs of those I serve.

Chapter Two describes the importance of shifting paradigms from Western to Chinese metaphors when working with Chinese American families. A brief overview of Chinese culture is presented to aid therapists in examining Chinese American families while taking into account their culture of origin, values, beliefs, and customs. Included in the chapter are a comparison of Chinese and Asian identities, a discussion of the traditional Chinese attitudes toward mental health, and an examination of the differences between Chinese and American perspectives.

The basic theory underpinning my model is discussed in Chapter Three. The concepts are based on values, beliefs, and customs derived from Buddhism, Taoism, and Confucianism. Case vignettes are used to describe how these concepts can be used to develop a therapeutic milieu that is meaningful and useful to Chinese American clients.

Chapter Four describes ways to integrate theoretical concepts from six models with Chinese concepts to provide a comprehensive multidimensional clinical approach; these models are (1) Structural Family Therapy, (2) Strategic Therapy, (3) Planned Short-Term Treatment, (4) Rational-Emotive Therapy, (5) Solution Focused Therapy, and (6) Contextual Family Therapy.

The therapeutic process from beginning to end is described in Chapters Five and Six. The initial interview is critical in establishing a foundation on which therapists and their clients can work together to resolve presenting problems. Chapter Five describes a comprehensive, efficient, and effective initial interview. The description covers (1) the initial interview as a method of cultural assessment, (2) the initial interview as the initial therapy session, (3) guidelines for the interview, and (4) establishment of the contract. The story of the Lee family is used to illustrate the concepts and principles of practice that are discussed.

It is important for therapists to guide their clients in achieving the goals that were established in the initial session. How this can be accomplished is discussed in Chapter Six. Topics include (1) maintaining affinity, (2) highlighting positive attributes and behaviors, (3) working in sequences, (4) developing themes, (5) working the dyad, and (6) completing homework assignments. The Lee family is again used to demonstrate the concepts presented.

The appropriate way to end therapy, which is extremely important to the treatment process, will also be discussed in Chapter Six. If this is not done correctly, the progress made and the goals accomplished can be destroyed. The issues discussed include (1) how to plan for and structure the final interview, (2) what happens if there is no closing session, (3) how to anchor changes, (4) how to empower the family, and (5) how to balance the ledger between therapists and their clients. The final session with the Lee family will elucidate the ideas discussed.

Chapters Seven through Eleven demonstrate the use of the model with five families. Chapter Seven tells the story of John Woo, a chronically depressed first-generation Chinese American. Complicating the case was the fact that he had been in treatment for a year before seeing me. My tasks, in this case, were to help John overcome his depression, reconcile the cultural differences between him and his parents, and integrate his Chinese and Western beliefs.

The story of Robert and Jill Wang, married for five years and with two children, is told in Chapter Eight. The couple was in crisis, with Jill threatening to leave if her husband did not make significant changes in addressing her emotional needs. Robert's expectations for the marriage were based on traditional Chinese attitudes while Jill's were Western. Behavioral interventions were used to help the couple to reconcile their differences and achieve marital integration.

Chapter Nine tells the story of Katherine Chow, an eleven-month-old girl who was seen in the emergency room for fractured legs. Her father was highly resistant to treatment, stating that he had done nothing wrong. This case illustrates work with a family in which both domestic violence and child abuse have occurred. Supportive, case management, and cognitive interventions were used to help Mrs. Chow to overcome her adversities, divorce her husband, and achieve family integration.

The story of Edward Liu, a thirty-six-year-old man unable to reconcile the differences between his American side and his Chinese upbringing, is told in Chapter Ten. Learning that his second wife had filed for a divorce, he attempted suicide. My task was to help Edward to escape from his emotional prison and retain his loyalty to his parents while honoring his own desires. Affective and cognitive restructuring interventions were used to assist him in achieving these objectives.

Chapter Eleven tells the story of the Ching family, who were seen in therapy because sixteen-year-old Sheryl could no longer manage her nineteen-year-old psychotic brother, Ronald. This case describes the reluctance of a family to disclose that one of its members has a serious mental disorder. My tasks in this case were to assist Mr. Ching in overcoming his resistance to having his son treated, help Sheryl provide reasonable support to her family, and develop a treatment program that would be helpful to Ronald.

The mental health, social service, and child welfare needs of Chinese Americans are addressed in Chapter Twelve. Included in the discussion is the way these needs are being met by current programs, the effectiveness of the programs, and the funding available to meet the needs.

When teaching, whether in the role of professor, workshop leader, or retreat director, I encourage participants to ask questions because I believe that those who ask questions benefit the most. They generally have thought about the issues they are raising and are therefore more receptive and likely to retain what is presented. I hope that you have many questions in mind and that I adequately address them in the book. I also hope that this book will stimulate further questions and ideas that lead to more research and writing on the topics presented.

Chapter One

My Journey

At the age of fifty-four, I consider myself a very fortunate man. I have a loving wife, two beautiful children and a grandchild, and wonderful friendships. I am proud of my ethnic heritage, grateful for my career in social work, blessed by my faith as a Roman Catholic, and nourished by my social and recreational activities. I owe my good fortune to the many people who have loved, supported, and guided me through my life's journey. I was born into a traditional Chinese family, was raised by African American foster parents, grew up in a Mexican American community, and lived and worked among various ethnic groups in different regions of the United States. I converted to Roman Catholicism and struggled before I was able to resolve deep insecurities. I was given wonderful educational and career opportunities and was provided with encouraging teachers, supportive mentors, and loving friends. Through the years I learned to integrate these life experiences, and I now enjoy inner peace and harmony.

Based on my own experience, I have taken the concept of *family integration* and made it the cornerstone of a new model for Chinese American Family Therapy (CAFT). Family integration consists of living peacefully and in consonance with one's family and treating relatives with warmth, kindness, and respect. It allows the mind, body, and spirit to be healthy, and therefore at rest. It also allows me to recognize my uniqueness, live a harmonious life, and understand my place in the world.

CAFT originates from a synthesis of my life experiences as a first-generation Chinese American, my understanding of Chinese culture, and my expertise with many family therapy models. It is a complex and comprehensive approach to working with traditional Chinese families that combines other useful, established approaches. The theoretical concepts on which it is based mirror values within the Chinese culture, especially reciprocity, adaptation, and integrity. These concepts are also reflected in the need for loyalty, respect, honor, self-efficacy, and altruism.

My family's story can serve to illustrate the typical Chinese American experiences with immigration, discrimination, and assimilation into American society. Our struggles to maintain family and communal cohesiveness parallel those of many other Chinese American families who have faced the need to work their way out of poverty, the intergenerational conflicts particular to immigrants and their first-generation descendants, and the difficulties of those who were born here in trying to develop a personal identity.

Origins

My father immigrated from China to the United States in 1925, at the age of twenty-one. One year later, he met my mother in a restaurant in San Francisco's Chinatown where she worked as a waitress. Her family, after having suffered a business failure, left China to rebuild their lives. My father and mother quickly fell in love, married, and proceeded to have a large family, beginning with Evie, followed by Martin, Steven, Elizabeth, Chester, Douglas, me, and my younger sister, Elaine.

My parents, like most of their generation, came to this country in poverty, but through their commitment to each other, perseverance, the support of friends, and their desire to make life better for their children, they achieved personal success by eventually owning a small business. To a large extent, we first-generation Chinese Americans owe what we have achieved to our parents' courage, hard work, and sacrifices.

My father entered the United States as a *paper son*, the name given to those who come into the country under a false name. At that time, Chinese immigrants, along with many Asians, were discriminated against by being excluded from entering the United States, forbidden to leave and reenter the country once they were here, and prohibited from becoming naturalized citizens. This was an effort on the part of special-interest groups to keep Chinese out of the country and force those who were already here to either leave or work under adverse conditions. The legal basis for these prohibitions was a series of exclusionary acts passed by Congress in the late 1800s and early 1900s. These problems did not change until 1965, when we were given equal immigration status with other nationalities.

Like many of his generation, the only way my father could immigrate to the United States was under the pretense of being the child of a Chinese American citizen. My real surname is Gee, not Jung. My father's life as a paper son began as a means of survival and became a pattern of living I did not fully face until halfway through my life.

Growing Up

In 1936, my parents moved from San Francisco to southern California to seek better job opportunities and because they wanted to be with friends. They lived and worked in Lincoln Heights, a predominantly Mexican American community located in East Los Angeles. Like many of his friends in the meat-packing industry, my father worked as a butcher, and my mother worked as a grocery store clerk.

To survive and support the family, my parents had to work long hours seven days a week. This left them no choice but to place Steve, Elizabeth, Chester, Douglas, Elaine, and me—all of their children but the two oldest, Evie and Martin—in foster homes. I was sent away in 1944 when I was only fourteen months old. Being so young, I was unable to understand either the long days and hard labor my parents faced or the emotional fatigue my mother had suffered when one of her children died during childbirth in the hospital. The family was gradually reunited after my father built a grocery store with living quarters on the second floor in 1945. I returned home in 1949, when I was five years old.

The placing of children in out-of-home substitute care because of financial duress is still a common practice in Hong Kong, but not here in the United States. My nephew's daughter Bo Bo, for example, is cared for by a nanny during the week while both parents work to support the family. She then visits her family on weekends and holidays. However, among poor, uneducated, and unskilled Chinese immigrants in the United States, the alienation and isolation within families resulting from these types of working conditions are still frequent occurrences.

Typically, in many Chinese American immigrant families, both parents have to work at menial jobs, often during odd hours, and some find themselves exploited as employees. A father, for example, may work as a waiter from 4:00 P.M. to 3:00 A.M. while his wife works in a sweatshop sewing garments, often at less than minimum wage, from 7:00 A.M. to 7:00 P.M. Illegal-immigrant status, pride, or ignorance prevents these parents from seeking public assistance. Children either become latchkey kids, left alone or under the supervision of an older sibling, or are cared for by grandparents or other relatives living in the home. Unfortunately, numerous problems are seen in therapy that arise from these types of circumstances.

Early Childhood

I was placed with Da and John, an African American couple. As I grew into childhood with this loving couple, they became part of my new identity. My five and a half years with them in their community were filled with memories of love, kindness, and understanding. I, like my father, had become another man's son in a new world with a different culture.

Da and John cared for several foster children in their old, whitewashed bungalow. My clearest memory of Da takes me back to a day when she found me crying on my old spring bed because Larry, another foster child, had done something to hurt me. Da picked me up and held me, comforting me in the silence of her arms as I lay my head on her shoulder and my cheek against the fabric of her soft, cotton dress. As she enveloped and protected me, I felt loved.

John cared for me in similar ways. He would often take me with him to the grocery or liquor store. He would set me up on the counter and give me a nickel to buy candy while he talked with the other men who were hanging out at the store. Once, when I was with John in his dilapidated garage, he picked me up and held me while he explained that mosquitoes had bitten my arms and legs, and now the bites were blistered red welts in danger of getting infected. Step by step, he told me how he would have to open and clean each one and then bandage it. That is what he did, slowly and carefully. His kindness kept me from being afraid. In those first years with Da and John, I learned the type of confidence that comes from being loved, which gave me the ability to face the many struggles ahead.

In a child's mind, changes can seem to happen without any transition and this is how it was for me when I was taken back to my parents' home. It seems as if one day I just woke up and found myself with my mother and father again, in their home above the grocery store. On that day, when I opened my eyes, I was standing by a butcher block in the back room of the market. Behind me was the staircase leading to the living room and bedrooms upstairs. In front of me and on the other side of the butcher-block table stood my mother. She was scolding and punishing me for something, though I don't know what. I remember her harsh eyes and the sound of her voice and the fact that she never held me. This soon characterized our relationship. I became extremely fearful of my parents and attempted to avoid them whenever possible.

I never saw Da and John again.

Returning Home

After five and a half years away from my family, I had to find a way back into their life and into my Chinese culture. My parents were very traditional, speaking primarily Chinese, observing traditional cultural events and holidays, and involving themselves in their family and their district associations. I spoke no Chinese and was totally unfamiliar with Chinese customs and traditions. Immediately, however, I was immersed in my family's lifestyle and, with it, Chinese culture. I soon learned my position and responsibilities in the home and through time I became familiar with the conventions and legacies of my heritage.

My father had the reputation of being honorable, fun-loving, and generous. He enjoyed being a butcher, taking pride in his skill and in the fact that his meat, which was always aged, was of the best quality. He was known for being supportive of friends and family. I recall Mr. Jimmy Gee, one of my father's closest friends, telling me how my father took him in when he needed temporary help. My father also cared for my two uncles when they were in need. Today I try to emulate his qualities and the values to which he adhered.

My mother was viewed as being a gracious hostess, loving wife, and caring friend. As a child, I delivered things she had made or baked to her friends in the neighborhood. She spent hours chatting with her many friends who came to visit her. She was a tireless worker, constantly doing the thousand-and-one tasks required of a wife and a mother.

The mutual love my parents experienced could easily be seen in the manner in which they interacted. My parents were totally devoted to each other through fifty-four years of married life. This devotion was reflected on one occasion when my mother was ill in the hospital and, in order to provide her comfort and support, my father slept on the floor by her bedside until he had to leave for work in the morning. But my brothers and sisters and I seldom interacted with my father, who worked twelve to fourteen hours a day, six days a week, with half a day off on Sundays. My mother, as is characteristic of a Chinese family, took most of the responsibility for my brothers and sisters and me with the help of my two older sisters. I did not understand my mother's harshness and came to believe that she did not love me. I thought that I either was adopted or had been found in a garbage can. Eventually, I grew a deep sense of shame, thinking that I was unwanted, stupid, defective, or bad.

Often I longed to be near my father, but I did not dare to get close to him. In the evenings, while he sat on the couch engrossed in watching wrestling, I sat on a three-legged stool by the side of the couch, just watching him in the green glow of the black-and-white television set. As the youngest son, quiet and hidden away in this dim corner of the room, I could not compete, so I sat there, still and silent for much of the rest of my childhood.

This silence allowed me to observe, to take special note of the fact that our home was wrapped in Chinese decor and we ate Chinese food, celebrated Chinese holidays, and frequently attended banquets and other Gee Family and Kow Kong District Association festivities. I had to go with my parents when they played mahjong on Sundays at their friends' homes. Our lives were so filled with Chinese tradition that my parents wanted us to speak and write Chinese, so I attended Chinese school for six years. When my oldest brother, Martin, married Camilla, they observed Chinese marital traditions in addition to having a Catholic ceremony. Because my parents were so ethnocentric, they warned us never to marry *lo fans*, or Caucasians. When my sister Elaine disregarded their wishes and married Robert, a Caucasian, at my mother's insistence my parents neither attended the wedding nor welcomed her family into their home. My sister never forgave my mother for that rejection.

I too felt that sense of rejection. Because I respected and admired my father, I was crushed when an accident led me to believe that he felt about me the same way I thought my mother did. One day, I accidentally set the television set on fire. While spanking me for this, my father muttered, "Your mother is right. You are no good." Those words ripped through my heart because they upheld my belief in the way my mother saw me. It made it worse that I now thought that my father felt the same way.

One Christmas, this belief that I was rejected and not a part of the family overwhelmed me. Because I had been hoping for a real present instead of the usual functional gifts like shirts and pants and socks, I took my package and hid in my dim corner of the room. I sat there, opening the present. When I found that it was clothing again, I decided to wall myself in, to hide, to protect myself from the rejection and pain that constantly haunted me. From then on, I recall having only two conversations with my parents before I left home at eighteen. Although I know now that my parents tried to provide me with a good family life, I was never happy living with them as a child.

Positive Influences

Even though I was insecure while growing up, several things helped me to live with my unhappiness and insecurity. First was my friendship with Art, which began in the second grade. Art was a first-generation Mexican American, but our cultural differences did not prevent us from becoming lifelong friends, sharing many adventures and wonderful times together. He was the youngest of eight children, intelligent, athletic, and sociable. While I went on to college, he developed a career in automobile mechanics and truck driving.

Today, Art and I visit and vacation together. My experiences with him and other close friends fostered an exposure to and appreciation of the Mexican American culture. It was the first of many other cultures with which I integrated and that I allowed to influence my philosophy regarding people, relationships, and spirituality.

The second positive influence was my fascination with nature films. Through them I learned to appreciate and value the natural beauty in the world as well as the lessons nature has to offer. Although I did not know it at that time, I was developing a natural affinity for and an integration with Taoism, whose philosophical precepts are often based in observation of nature. Once I was on my own, I became an avid outdoors person.

A third positive factor in my life was learning to escape the hardships of daily life by daydreaming. My dreams were always associated with being the best at whatever I undertook and finding love and happiness in the future. I learned that dreams can come true, and that often the role of a therapist is to help immigrant families fulfill the hopes and dreams they have brought to this country.

The fourth positive factor was a strong religious experience. This happened after I was baptized a Roman Catholic at St. Bridget's, a mission church in Chinatown in Los Angeles. At twelve, I had a profound religious experience. While listening to the Sermon on the Mount during mass at Sacred Heart Catholic Church in Lincoln Heights, I felt that Christ was speaking directly to me. I began crying and immediately felt loved, special, and worthwhile. Throughout my adolescence, I continued to listen attentively to the Epistle and Gospel readings. I learned to avoid judging others, to forgive those who injured me, and to be charitable without asking for recognition or rewards. I also learned to treat others with respect and to be aware that everyone was a brother or a sister to me. Finally, the readings helped me to understand the meaning and importance of suffering and the need to care for the poor and disenfranchised. I am sure that the latter awareness led me to major in social work as an undergraduate.

Although this experience did change my external attitude, my relationship with my parents remained much the same. This was an internal change or transforming experience. Before, I had felt unloved and unwanted, with no special qualities. Afterward, I felt loved, wanted, and very special. This special feeling was not related to anything specific (what I call *form*) but was internal (that is, *substance*). I still thought I was clumsy and stupid, but when I experienced God's love, I felt special. A seed had been planted that affirmed my true self; this allowed me to begin changing my negative self-perceptions and, through the years, it permitted me to accept the skills and attributes that I possessed but that were never recognized and validated by my parents.

Later, as an adult, I found it easy to accept my Catholicism and integrate it with Confucianism, because on a substantive level they are similar. Both, for example, regard devotion, compassionate love, and justice, as paramount virtues. My appreciation and acceptance of these Western and Eastern spiritual views has helped me to work equally effectively with both Caucasian and Chinese American families.

Junior and Senior High School

My life became easier and more enjoyable when I entered Abraham Lincoln Junior and Senior High School. Even though this school's student body was overwhelmingly Mexican American and had a reputation for being overrun with gangs, I had many friends, participated in various sports, joined many clubs, and was elected to several class offices. One of my favorite teachers, Mr. Lopez, encouraged me and taught me organizational and planning skills that I still use today. But though I began to try more, to do more, and to stay busy, this did not always work well for me.

In the seventh grade, I became an obnoxious class clown to hide my bad feelings about myself. My behavior attracted the attention I needed, but it was negative attention. During my social studies class, I interrupted a student and made a sarcastic remark. The teacher embarrassed me in front of everyone, and though she did not know it, she exposed one of my worst fears—being stupid, or being seen as stupid. I felt so humiliated that for nearly thirty years, I never voluntarily raised a question in a class or group situation.

In junior and senior high school I joined the chess club, edited the annual, wrote for the school newspaper, played linebacker on the football team, and joined the gymnastics, cross-country, and track teams in addition to keeping up with my regular studies and responsibilities at home. In spite of all this, I remained painfully shy and introverted and needed immense support and encouragement from teachers and friends. I lived under the constant fear that someone would discover that I was insecure, defective, and hypocritical. Staying busy helped me to hide under the cover of fulfilling responsibilities, hoping that someone would accept me and acknowledge me for my many accomplishments.

Eventually, I became student body president. I hoped my parents would be proud of me for this accomplishment. Instead, on the day I was elected, my mother told my second-oldest sister, Liz, that the only reason I ran for the office was to show off. Hearing this, I felt devastated. I realized that I could do nothing to please her, so I decided to leave home and move in with my second-oldest brother, Steve, and his wife, Hazel, immediately after graduation. When I told my parents of my decision, my mother tried to tell me that she had treated me fairly. But I was surprised when my father began crying, telling me that he cared for me and that he worked hard so I could have a better life than he had. At that moment, I finally felt that they loved me. Nevertheless, I knew I had to leave.

The junior and senior high school years can be very difficult times for Chinese American adolescents. We are often expected by our parents and teachers to go on to college, to become high achievers, and to get involved in extracurricular activities. Many students, however, do not have the ability or aptitude to meet these expectations. Frequently, instead of supporting and encouraging their children in directions where they may succeed, parents are out of touch with the children's feelings. As a result, Chinese American parents can become critical, punitive, and unreasonable in their demands, which often leads to adolescent rebellion. I was fortunate to be able to meet my parents' expectations for me, but my accomplishments did nothing to improve my home life or sense of security.

Early Marriage, Finding a Calling, and Education

I was introduced to Rosie, who is also a first-generation Chinese American, at the age of sixteen by my brother Steve. Although I took some time to date others, most of whom were not Chinese, Rosie and I discovered at nineteen that we wanted to spend the rest of our lives together. Both families disapproved of our plans to marry, believing we were too young.

Nevertheless, we were married on May 8, 1964, at the age of twenty. We lived just west of downtown Los Angeles, near Third Street and Vermont Avenue. Like most young couples, we experienced many difficulties in the beginning of our marriage. In 1965, we separated, but shortly afterward we reconciled because of parental pressure and the feelings of guilt we experienced for having abandoned our families and inflicting shame on them.

The birth of our son, Richard, and later our daughter, Eileen, were joyful events; however, the year that followed was extremely stressful. Both Rosie and I were employed full-time as clerk-typists for the City of Los Angeles. Typing was the only skill I had learned in high school. I initially worked for the police department and later transferred to the library, where I could have flexible hours to attend college. I attended junior college four nights a week, with the hope of someday becoming a history teacher. Fortunately, Po Po and Gon Gon (meaning grandfather and grandmother on the wife's side of the family) lived close by and were able to care for the children while we worked. Later, when the children were old enough, they were enrolled in a nearby day care program.

In many respects, my marriage to Rosie mirrors my parents' traditional relationship. We are devoted to our children, with Rosie taking the major responsibility for their upbringing. We celebrate important events and both work to support our family and improve our lives. We also continue to be involved in our extended families and cultural activities. Finally, in the same way that my mother supported my father's goals, Rosie has always supported my personal aspirations and career objectives.

Finding a Calling

The next few years were relatively uneventful, with our family life fairly peaceful. We both continued to work while Rosie's parents watched our children. I began attending school full-time, and in my junior year I made a decision that changed the course of my studies and my life.

While I was sitting in a Russian history class in my junior year at California State University, Los Angeles, my daydreaming lifted me away from the lecture. I began once again to plan and figure my credits, checking and rechecking to see how long it would be before I had completed my major in history. There I sat in the fourth seat in the fourth row, staring at the green chalkboard, trying to imagine standing in front of a class, and once again I felt too afraid to speak. If I continued my major in history, I would have to speak in front of classes all the time. At that point in my life, I believed this to be impossible, so as I watched the professor lecturing to the forty to fifty students in my classroom, I changed my mind and thought about finding a new major.

I briefly reflected on what I might enjoy doing. I recalled always wanting to be a Good Samaritan by helping the disadvantaged and underprivileged. Concluding that social work would allow me to fulfill this desire, I quickly decided to change my major. I was totally unaware of what social workers actually provided and what the field offered. Nevertheless, from that moment on, doors began opening for me. In my first welfare class, my instructor told me to do some volunteer work to figure out what I was doing. A friend who worked with gangs found a volunteer position for me as group counselor in a program devoted to working with predelinquent Mexican American and African American adolescents.

During my senior year, I received excellent training as a group counselor from an organization called Special Service For Groups. More importantly, however, through my exposure to community groups in East Los Angeles and Watts, I learned about the devastating effects of discrimination and institutional racism on the lives of individuals and communities. I learned that I was working with many adolescents whose problems were caused in part by the discriminatory policies and procedures in the schools they attended and the lack of adequate support from health and welfare agencies. My experiences led me to develop a social conscience and to know that if I was accepted into graduate school, I wanted to specialize in community organization. I no longer wanted to focus on working with individuals but with the institutions that negatively influence those individuals.

Following graduation, I worked a year for the Los Angeles County Probation Department as a camp counselor. It was a nice break from school. Then, in 1969, I was accepted into the University of Southern California's Graduate School of Social Work. Even though I was awarded a full scholarship and a living stipend, I still felt stupid and insecure. However, these feelings gradually began to change with the support and encouragement I received from faculty and friends. My two years at USC were the happiest I spent in college.

Working with the Asian American Movement

While in graduate school, I was asked to join the Asian American movement, also known as the Asian and Pacific Islander movement. My immediate response was to say no, because I thought I had nothing in common with the members of other Asian groups. But after a great deal of reflection, I reversed my decision for the following reasons. First, I concluded that although the Asian American movement had several problems, I could accept the thought of "Asian American" as a political concept; however, I still have not been able to accept it culturally or as a way to identify myself. Second, I recognized the fact that unless they are brought to the attention of political officials, the health, mental health, social, and child welfare needs of Asian American groups would continue to be unmet. Third, I believed that my participation could fulfill my desire to help bring about necessary institutional changes. Fourth, I believe that every citizen has a civic responsibility to contribute to the betterment of his or her community. Participating in the Asian American movement would help me to fulfill that responsibility. Finally, while reflecting on whether or not to join the Asian American movement, I realized that I had unknowingly internalized the values that had been lived and taught by my parents. I felt an affinity toward my Chinese heritage and, like my father, a strong obligation to help Chinese Americans.

The Asian American movement initially focused on helping Asian groups to become visible, be politically active, and acquire a voice. Among our activities, we educated national and state government officials regarding the mental health and social service needs of Asian Americans, advocated for programs to meet those needs, and organized groups to help identify and rectify problems in our communities. Although there is still much more to do, Asian Americans are now visible, have a voice, are involved in all levels of politics, and are seeing to it that their educational, health, mental health, social, and child welfare needs are being met.

Graduate School

While a friend and fellow graduate student and I were doing some research work at USC, we began working on a pilot project that required us to travel to various graduate schools. These schools were so impressed with our initiative that three of them asked me to apply to their doctoral programs. Eventually I accepted a full scholarship at the University of Pennsylvania (UP).

While at UP, I developed an interest in knowing about my Chinese culture, so I took courses in the Asian Studies Department. The more I learned, the more I appreciated my cultural heritage and understood my parents' attitudes and behaviors. During this period I also became very active in Philadelphia's Chinese community and helped to establish the first Asian American organization in the city, the Asian American Council of Greater Philadelphia. Membership in the Council included mental health and social service professionals, educators, ministers, and businesspeople. Its major objectives were to help in identifying and rectifying the health, mental health, education, and social service needs of Asian Americans in Philadelphia.

Integrating Work and Family Life

I had planned to work for the National Institute of Mental Health upon my graduation from UP in 1973. Instead, I was recruited by the Hahnemann Medical College and Hospital in Philadelphia and became an assistant professor and an outpatient clinic director. Hahnemann, which is located near the center of the city, served several ethnic communities, most of whom were extremely poverty-stricken.

The hospital's community mental health center emphasized professional growth, and by using the faculty of the hospital, I received training in a variety of treatment models. These included intensive psychotherapy for children and adults, sex therapy, play therapy, and dance therapy. Our service area also allowed me to become familiar with the customs and values of several ethnic groups with which I had been unfamiliar. During this period I was instrumental in establishing the first outpatient mental health clinic in Philadelphia's Chinatown. It was also during this period that I received my family therapy training, first in Contextual Family Therapy and later in Structural Family Therapy and Strategic Therapy with Salvador Minuchin and Jay Haley.

Reconciliation with My Family

While working at Hahnemann Medical College and Hospital, I was influenced by Ivan Boszormenyi-Nagy, originator of Contextual Family Therapy. He convinced me of the importance of reconciling my differences with my parents. With his support and guidance, I made several visits home to make peace with them. From our conversations, I learned about their friendships, the devotion they had toward one another, and the many struggles with which they had been confronted. My father, for example, like many other Chinese, had to overcome a serious gambling problem. My mother had a terror of being in hospitals; on more than one occasion, she had nearly died in childbirth. My parents had to support not only us, but my mother's family as well. Our talks led me to love and care for them and they, in turn, learned to admire and respect me.

Earlier in my life, I had rebelled. I discounted my parents' advice about maintaining my Chinese heritage when I began to identify myself as an American instead of a Chinese American. Even though I rebelled against my cultural heritage, I think it was more a rebellion against my mother and her rigid positions. I have found this to be true of many Chinese adolescents with whom I have worked. At some level, I have always been ethnocentric. Reconciling with my parents only helped to increase that ethnocentricity.

I viewed my six years in Philadelphia as a major transitional period. It was a time of integration. I overcame many insecurities that had plagued me throughout my childhood, made peace with my parents, and acquired the knowledge and skills I needed to grow professionally. I continued to learn about and deepen my connection with my Chinese heritage. I gained insights regarding my talents and felt secure in meeting the challenges I would face. Most importantly, I once again developed a loving relationship with Rosie.

Going Home

Rosie and I were fond of Philadelphia; we had many friends from varied backgrounds, enjoyed our work, and found immense satisfaction in participating in the Chinese community. However, we missed our families, and being Chinese, we wanted our children to be influenced by their grandparents. In 1976, we moved to Riverside, California, where I became executive director of the Family Service Association of Riverside (FSAR).

Assuming the directorship of FSAR was the perfect job opportunity, allowing me to use the clinical, organizational, and teaching skills I had acquired in Philadelphia to redirect an agency in crisis and help it to more fully meet the needs of the community it served. I enjoyed working with the board of directors, staff, and colleagues from other United Way agencies. I also enjoyed being part of the family service movement, which included nearly three hundred other family service agencies located throughout the United States and Canada.

Visiting China

In 1984, when my mother died at the age of seventy-three, my father honored me by asking me to give the eulogy at her funeral. Normally that privilege is given to an older friend of the family. A great deal of reflection went into the eulogy because I wanted to be honest and sincere in what I expressed. I conferred with my brothers and sisters and my mother's brothers to incorporate their thoughts and experiences. While delivering the eulogy, I cried and felt a closeness with her.

Soon after my mother's death, I learned that my father had been married previously and had a son and three grandsons living in Hong Kong. It was not uncommon in my parents' generation for men to have two wives, one in China and one in the United States. Until 1943, many of the Chinese immigrants to the United States were men who lived alone and sent money back to China to support their families there. They were lonely and naturally wanted companionship. Rosie's uncle and grandfather also had more than one wife.

According to Chinese custom, polygamy was an accepted practice as long as all the wives were supported. My father's first marriage had been arranged, and while he was married to my mother he continued to support his other family. His first wife had died in 1947 and the care of the children was given to a nanny. After my mother's death, I went with him to visit his birthplace in China and met my half-brother and his family, with whom I later became very close. The trip was one of my most beautiful and memorable experiences.

My full awareness and acceptance of my ancestry happened on this first trip to China with my father. We arrived in Beijing in the evening and before dawn I was walking the streets. As the sun rose and people began filling the streets, I suddenly and unexpectedly became overwhelmed with emotions. I felt connected to all the people who surrounded me; I felt a part of the city, the country, and its history. I felt enveloped by the entire Chinese culture, and I was so overwhelmed that I began crying intensely. At that moment, I felt I had returned home, and the sense of pride I experienced was beyond description. It was another *peak*, or integrative experience.

We spent a month touring the country. What I had studied about Chinese culture came alive. I saw the diversity of China's land, each region with its own beauty. I observed the diversity of its people, with their different languages, foods, customs, and dress. I learned about its history, with its ancient temples, gardens, and sacred places. And I experienced its countless art forms, including calligraphy, scroll paintings, opera, ivory carving, and silk weaving. My ethnic pride deepened with each day's journey.

The following year I took Rosie, our children, and her family to visit her father's family and birthplace. Later we toured the country and, as I had the year before, they too had a wonderful and profound experience. My children's ethnic pride deepened as a result of that trip, and they told me later that they would only marry someone Chinese. They kept their word. I believe that their decision was influenced not only by our trip, but also by the strong ethnocentricity they have seen in Rosie and me; the strong influence of their grandparents, whom they love dearly; and the exposure to Chinese American culture they have had throughout their lives.

Professional Development

Initially I planned to remain in the family service movement and to direct a larger agency in the southern California area. However, I began to develop a stronger attraction to clinical practice and to teaching and training in the area of marital and family therapy.

In 1984, I left FSAR to develop a clinic and training institute in San Bernardino with three colleagues. Unfortunately, we were unsuccessful, so in 1986, I entered private practice, in addition to being an adjunct professor at both the University of Southern California, Graduate School of Social Work, and Loma Linda University Graduate Department of Family and Counseling Science; I also provided workshops and in-service training to social service, family service, Asian American, and mental health organizations throughout the southwestern United States. My first book, *Constructual Marital Therapy*, was published in 1993. The following year I accepted a full-time teaching position with the California State University, San Bernardino, Graduate Department of Social Work, where I am today. I continue to have a small private practice and provide workshops and in-service training programs.

Since leaving FSAR in 1984, I have added new models of practice to those I learned in Philadelphia. These include Emotionally Focused, Solution Focused, Rational-Emotive, and Behavioral Therapy. I have learned—through teaching, writing, supervising, and training—to integrate these models in a manner that allows me to match a model or combine models to meet the unique problems, needs, and characteristics of the families I serve in treatment.

My Father's Death

With all the family gathered around his bedside, my father died at the age of eighty-seven in 1991. As in life, his death brought the family together in a loving union. We loved him dearly, and although we experienced tremendous grief, his passing was an intimate time. We were able to release him from this life with joy because he was ready. He wanted to be with my mom again. I could see this in his eyes.

My granddaughter, Brittany Elizabeth Jung, was born on February 10, 1997. She is part of the third generation of Chinese Americans in our family. Her future success will fulfill part of my parents' dreams.

My Perspective

My journey has taught me that there are many paths to seeking and discovering spiritual, psychological, and emotional fulfillment. My life has also taught me to appreciate and value different lifestyles, cultural beliefs, and religious practices along with recognizing that everyone needs loving and supportive relationships to overcome fears, address adversity, and cultivate a fulfilling and prosperous life. My experiences have also prepared me for my various professional roles and led me to develop my unique model, Chinese American Family Therapy.

For me, life has been a process of integration. I learned to integrate and heal the emotional wounds of my childhood by finding peace with my parents. I learned to integrate the early conflicts in my marriage by relinquishing angry and resentful feelings and focusing instead on what was good and loving in our relationship. My exposure to various ethnic communities has allowed me to admire and accept the good every culture has to offer. My understanding of Catholicism, Confucianism, Taoism, and Buddhism has allowed me to integrate the beauty each has to offer into an eclectic philosophical view of life. Finally, my comprehension of various clinical models has permitted me to integrate them into a varied approach for working with families in therapy.

As with all immigrant families, my parents' task was to integrate and find peace in their adopted country. Even though they were confronted with the typical adversities faced by immigrants, including discrimination, financial hardship, and intergenerational conflicts, they were able to achieve their dreams and provide a home life that allowed their children and grandchildren to succeed in taking advantage of the opportunities this country has to offer. Their success was the result of their ability to adapt to their host culture while honoring their own cultural values of reciprocity, loyalty, respect, honor, self-efficacy, and altruism. The use of these concepts in treating traditional immigrant parents and their children will be addressed in Chapter Three.

My parents, for the most part, adjusted to the American culture rather than becoming assimilated into it. They identified with being Chinese, and their primary cultural, social, recreational, and psychological needs were met within the Chinese community. They carried their culture of origin with them.

I, on the other hand, like others belonging to the first generation in America, have had to integrate aspects of both Chinese and American culture. I was able to accomplish this by accepting, knowing, and taking pride in my ethnic heritage. As a therapist, I recognized that to deny my Chinese heritage would be to deny my very existence. Once I accepted my ethnicity, I could select from it and from the broader culture the elements that were meaningful and enhancing and disregard those that were meaningless and detracting.

This is one of the most important principles of CAFT. In therapy, family members are helped to recognize that when they take and integrate what is good from both Chinese and American cultures, diversity can solve rather than create problems. It can strengthen family cohesiveness, and it can promote healthy adaptation to this country.

Chapter Two

A Paradigm Shift

From Western to Chinese Culture

In Chapter One, I described my personal journey as a first-generation Chinese American and the obstacles I had to overcome to find the peace I now experience. It is time now to look at the bigger picture and pursue the goal of this book, which is to present a new counseling model for working with Chinese Americans. We first need to understand that the objective of all family therapy is to assist families in resolving the issues they bring to treatment. This requires an understanding not only of the problems themselves, whether they relate to oppositional behavior, drug abuse, or schizophrenia, but of numerous other issues, including intrapersonal and family dynamics, stages of family development, and communication patterns. The theories and models of practice that provide this understanding must also be sensitive to the cultural context of the families seeking services; otherwise, problems and issues will be misdiagnosed, interventions unsuitable, and treatment ineffective.

Thus, the treatment of immigrant Chinese families must be examined from a Chinese, rather than an Asian or Western, perspective. This chapter provides information that allows this to be accomplished. It will begin with a discussion of issues related to having either a Chinese or an Asian identity, followed by a brief overview of Chinese culture. The chapter proceeds with an analysis of the importance of family and community in Chinese culture, differences among Chinese, and traditional Chinese attitudes toward mental health. It concludes with an in-depth description of several differences between Chinese and American viewpoints.

Chinese Versus Asian Identity

The Asian American concept has been used very effectively in gathering census data, establishing and maintaining a political base for various Asian groups, and identifying and addressing the educational, employment, housing, health, mental health, and social service needs of Asian Americans, as well as in lobbying for programs and services to meet them. However, the "melting pot" concept allows for the misuse of statistical data, which can be misleading in identifying and addressing the various needs within each Asian group. It overlooks the uniqueness of each ethnic group under its umbrella and minimizes the problems Asian groups have toward one another.

The Asian American concept is also paradoxical, since it goes contrary to the belief of the leaders of the Asian American movement in "cultural pluralism," a concept that recognizes and honors the uniqueness of ethnic groups. The fact is that not all Asians are alike, nor are they one homogenous group. Therefore, not only is the concept misleading but, as Fong and Mokuau (1994) point out, ignoring the heterogeneity of each Asian group leads to programs and interventions based on general principles that may be useful, effective, or meaningful for only one group. Because of their cultural, religious, and philosophical differences, for example, therapeutic interventions for Chinese families founded on the principles of Confucianism, Taoism, and Buddhism would not be appropriate for Asian Indians, whose beliefs are founded on Hinduism and Sikhism, or Filipinos, whose culture is heavily influenced by Roman Catholicism.

According to the 1990 census, 7,273,662 Asians and Pacific Islanders live in the United States. As indicated in Table 2.1, the large majority, 84.2 percent, are represented by Chinese, Filipinos, Japanese, Asian Indians, Koreans, and Vietnamese. Statistics on these populations are often generalized to the remainder of the nearly thirty groups. Asians are considered to be model minorities because statistics on Chinese American households' annual income, which exceeds that of their Caucasian counterparts, are generalized to all Asian Americans. However, the annual incomes of many of the other Asian or Pacific Islander groups are near or below the poverty line.

By projecting a picture of harmony and unity, the concept also distorts reality and obscures many of the major conflicts, some of which go back for centuries, between various Asian groups. For example, in several areas within Asia, conflicts between different cultures define distinctions between the various groups: the Chinese are ruthlessly decimating Tibet; between 1978 and 1980, hundreds of thousands of Chinese were forced to leave Vietnam because of the anti-Chinese sentiment toward them (Freeman, 1995), and many Chinese harbor tremendous animosity toward Japanese because of the atrocities the Japanese committed toward them, their family members, or friends during World War II.

Table 2.1. Population Counts of the Largest Asian or Pacific Islander Groups in the United States, 1990.

Ethnic Group	Population	Percentage
Chinese	1,645,472	22.6
Filipino	1,406,770	19.3
Japanese	847,562	11.7
Asian Indian	815,447	11.2
Korean	798,849	11.0
Vietnamese	614,547	8.4
Cambodian	417,411	5.7
Hawaiian	211,014	2.9
Lao	149,014	2.1
Thai	91,275	1.3
Hmong	90,082	1.2
Samoan	62,964	0.9
Guamanian	49,345	0.7
Others	73,410	1.0

Source: Asians in America, p. 96.

Despite efforts to homogenize Asian identities for various reasons, major differences exist that must be accepted for family therapy to be successful. This is why I developed a therapeutic model that is uniquely suited to meeting the needs of Chinese Americans. Although some concepts can be applied to other groups, the model respects, preserves, and takes into consideration the rich and unique characteristics of Chinese and their culture.

Chinese Culture

Studying the Chinese people in their historical context reveals how Chinese personal identity is influenced by and interwoven with being part of a communal society. Chinese are extremely proud of their history and are intricately joined with it. This is evident in their countless traditions, their doctrine of ancestor worship, and their belief in Confucianism, a philosophy based on ancient Chinese customs and beliefs.

Chinese culture had its beginnings along the Yellow River on the North China Plain and in its continuous small river valleys (Reischauer and Fairbank, 1960). Historians date Chinese prehistory somewhere between 4000 and 2700 B.C. (Eberhard, 1971). The realm of history, however, begins with the Shang dynasty (c. 1600–1028 B.C.). Chinese culture evolved through a series of dynasties, some lasting a very short period of time and others lasting thousands of years, the last one being the Manchu dynasty (1644–1911). China became a republic under the leadership of Sun Yat-sen in 1912, but this period lasted only until 1948 when, under the leadership of Mao Tse-tung's Communist regime, China became what it remains today, the People's Republic of China.

China has never been one homogenous society but instead includes five separate cultural and economic regions: China proper, Manchuria, Mongolia, Xinjiang Uygur, and Tibet. It is a multinational country made up of a large number of ethnic groups. Although the official language is Mandarin, the Chinese language, depending on the region, is divided into several mutually unintelligible languages, as distinct from each other as Spanish is from Italian. Within these languages are many dialects. For example, the first immigrants to the United States were Cantonese-speaking Chinese from Guangdong, a province located in southeast China. Today, however, there has been a large influx of Mandarin-speaking immigrants from both northern China and Taiwan. As a result, we now have neighbors, television stations, and films in both Mandarin and Cantonese all around us in the United States.

Chinese civilization, like any other culture, is more than language, values, traditions, and history; it also includes dress, literature, politics, economics, architecture, and etiquette—everything connected to the Chinese people's lives. However, for the purposes of this book, I will focus my discussion on Chinese religion and philosophy, the foundations upon which Chinese values, beliefs, and codes of conduct have evolved.

Unlike most Westerners, who adhere to a monotheistic religion where people pray to one God for all their spiritual needs, Chinese have had a polytheistic tradition, based on local folklore, superstition, and magical practices and beliefs, in which people pray to different gods for different purposes. This is indicated by the variety of temples, shrines, and altars found in Chinese cities and villages. Chen-wu, for example, was the god of the northern sky, who was called upon to protect the community from banditry and crimes. T'ai'shan was the mountain god, who was believed to have authority over both the present life and the afterlife. He was one of the gods responsible for judging sinful conduct. Another god was Kuan Yu, who was worshiped by merchants as a god of wealth and protector of business contracts, by common people as a healer of disease, and by many communities as the chief protective deity against calamities and destruction (Yang, 1961).

According to Yang, "For the common people, the dominant purpose of religion was its magical value in obtaining happiness and warding off evil. Magic allowed for achieving tangible results in a particular situation. It contained no moral dogma of universal validity for social life. As such, magic placed no opposition to the practicing of secular moral values. Hence, a common man could worship a Buddhist god for the general happiness of himself and his family, pray to a Taoist deity for the return of his health, and at the same time practice Confucian morality" (p. 283). This functional use of religion reflects the Chinese people's pragmatic approach to life, which, as I will describe later, has assisted many Chinese immigrants in adapting to their adopted country.

It is essential for mental health professionals to understand the three major belief systems in Chinese culture if they are going to effectively treat traditional Chinese families. These religions continue to be the dominant factors influencing Chinese family and communal life, which is the foundation of Chinese society. They also shape the Chinese people's views toward health, mental health, and family wellness as well as guiding them toward the resolution of problems in these areas.

Confucianism

Confucianism, which dominated the system of social values in China for nearly two thousand years, was not religion, but a certain philosophy toward life and the universe. Confucius (551–479 B.C.) was a social reconstructionist who arrived in China during a period of moral, political, and economic decay. His importance lies in the fact that he systematized a body of ideas that were not of his own creation and communicated them to a circle of disciples. His teachings were later set down in writing and formed the moral code of the upper classes of China.

Confucius believed that for China to reverse itself and restore peace and order, people must turn to the lessons of the past that required individuals to play their proper, assigned roles in a fixed society of hierarchical authority. Thus, his vision of society, and particularly of the family, was highly structured and hierarchical. It clearly defined roles for everyone. This was reflected in his five famous relationships: ruler and subject, father and son, husband and wife, elder brother and younger brother, and friend and friend. The hier-

archical nature of his rules for governing these relationships was explicit: the individual was subordinated to the group, the young to the
aged, the living to the ancestors, the wife to the husband, the children to the parents, and the daughter-in-law to the mother-in-law.

Confucius's intent was not to establish a society and family life
based simply upon rigid rules and regulations. Instead, relationships
were to be based upon moral principles that applied to everyone.
Principles such as justice, compassion, and love were to be followed
in all situations. He believed that these principles were the will of
heaven for human beings. Ethical people were to be honest, frugal,
industrious, and willing to contribute to the welfare of the family
and society.

Confucian philosophy, sometimes called ethical humanism,
emphasized concern for humanity and human nature. Relationships
were to be mutual and reciprocal, based upon fairness, honor, and
respect. There was to be justice between father and son, not just
blind obedience. Likewise, there was to be prudent reserve between
spouses, respect between brothers, and sincerity between friends. If
individuals performed their functions and roles in a perfunctory
manner, without integrity, they were considered to be hypocritical.
This is reflected in the following three proverbs found in *The Analects of Confucius*, a book of Confucian precepts (Waley, 1938):

1. Tzu-yu asked about the treatment of parents. The Master said,
   "Filial sons nowadays are people who see to it that their parents get enough to eat. But even dogs and horses are cared for
   to that extent. If there is no feeling of respect, wherein lies the
   difference?" [p. 89]

2. The Master said, "Man's very life is honesty, in what without it
   he will be lucky indeed if he escapes with his life" [p. 118]

3. The Master said, "Respect the young. How do you know that
   they will not one day be all that you are now? But if a man has
   reached forty or fifty and nothing has been heard of him, then
   I grant there is no need to respect him" [p. 143]

Thus, Confucius envisioned a society and family life knitted together by norms for social conduct that reflected personal virtues of love, integrity, loyalty, sincerity, and benevolence. These virtues were often demonstrated in various family and communal rites and rituals. To honor and live by Confucian doctrines was to earn respect. Not doing so engendered shame, not only for the individual, but for the family and ancestors as well. Thus, personal conduct in China is governed by shame rather than guilt, as it is in Western society.

Taoism

Taoism, both a philosophy and a religion, dates back to the time of Confucius and was in the beginning a protest or rebellion against the growing despotism of rules and the growing rigidity of the time. Where the Confucian moralists sought to bring individuals into conformity with social norms, the Taoists emphasized the independence of the individual and conformity to the patterns of nature. This pattern of nature was the Tao, or the Way. According to Reischauer and Fairbank (1960, p. 74), "The Tao is founded on a nameless, formless 'non-being'; it 'cannot be heard,' 'cannot be seen,' and 'cannot be spoken.' But it is, in essence, the totality of the natural processes to which man must conform. Despite constant flux, the Tao is unitary, having no distinctions of big or little, high or low, life or death, good or bad. The relativity of all things and the dependence of any quality on its opposite are constant Taoist themes."

The Taoist themes of relativity and opposites are illustrated in Chapter Two of the *Tao Te Ching* (English and Feng, 1972), a book attributed to Lao-tzu (c. 604–c. 514 B.C.):

The Taoists believed that the various theories of improving the world only made things worse because they all depended on telling other people what to do. According to them, things were fine in their natural state and should be left alone; this included plants, animals, and people. Thus, Taoist philosophy was one of nonaction. This did not imply a lack of action; instead, it implied action without insincerity, overreacting, or attachment to the action itself. The emphasis was on finding harmony with the natural order of things, rather than trying to change it. The ideal condition for Taoists would be to never leave their home and to find peace in their village.

There were four major streams of Taoism. They all emphasized themes of passivity, individuality, discovery of peace and harmony in nature, asceticism, and the search for immortality. Taoism also had a mystical element, with secret initiation rites, practices in Yoga, and breathing exercises for achieving trances. However, unlike Western mysticism, which has focused on identification with a personal God, the Taoists stressed the union of the individual with an impersonal natural order (Welch, 1965).

Taoism remained popular in Chinese culture because it complemented Confucianism. The latter emphasized a morality based on conformity to the group and to many rigid cultural norms, thereby stifling individuality, creativity, and aceticism. Taoism met the needs of the many Chinese who required such freedoms. The Taoist influence on Chinese culture can be seen not only in the manner in which the Chinese conducted their lives, but also in their artistic and poetic expression. In traditional Chinese landscape painting, for example, the people are always subordinate to the scenery.

Buddhism

Siddhartha Gautama, his name before he became Buddha ("the Enlightened One"), was born about 560 B.C. in a border district on the northeastern Gangetic plain near the Himalayan foothills in India. He was born into a rich, royal Brahman family. According to legend, he was spoiled and sheltered from the ills of the time. However, once he had been exposed to poverty and disease, he left the comfort of his princely life in search of enlightenment, first by living a life of extreme asceticism and later through spiritual guidance, discipline, and cultivation of meditative trances. What he learned on his journey to enlightenment became the foundation upon which Buddhist moral dogmas, traditions, and rituals are built (Robinson and Johnson, 1982).

Buddhism was the dominant religion in China from the middle of the fourth century to the end of the eighth century. It appeared in China during the late Han dynasty (A.D. 25–220), a time when there was much disillusionment and upheaval in China. This was the result of both internal problems and strife related to warring tribes that invaded the country. In these troubled times, the Chinese needed spiritual uplifting, something the popular sects of Taoism were unable to satisfy. Buddhism had much to offer, including literature, a beautiful religious art, aesthetically satisfying ceremonies, the appeal of a peaceful monastic life in a troubled time, and the promise of personal salvation at a time when life seemed hopeless (Ch'en, 1973).

The Buddhist religion has many moral dogmas and principles that guide its followers to reach Nirvana, the peaceful state in the absence of desire, for example, Buddha's four noble truths and noble eightfold path. However, Buddha's major guiding rules were "not to commit any evil, to do good, and to purify one's own mind" (Ch'en, 1973, p. 6). The Chinese were attracted to the Mahayana form of Buddhism, which supported piety for all creatures and salvation for all humanity as the only possible means of achieving personal salvation, as opposed to the Hinayana school, which emphasized the salvation of the individual. Both schools of Buddhism stressed the concept of cause and effect. Although it has been popular for centuries, Buddhism failed to change the fundamental way in which the Chinese viewed the world. Eventually, like Taoism, it was largely accommodated to those ingrained views.

The influence of Confucianism, Taoism, and Buddhism on traditional Chinese immigrants to the United States can easily be recognized, particularly in communities such as Monterey Park in Los Angeles County or San Francisco's Chinatown, which have large numbers of immigrants. The Confucian virtue of family loyalty and cohesiveness is still emphasized and is evidenced by the Chinese restaurants that are noisily filled with families having lunch or dinner or celebrating a wedding or the birth of a new child. Emphasis is still placed on respect and care for the elderly and observance of various rituals and traditions. Chinese funerals based on traditional religious practices are commonplace and individuals still pray to different gods for favors. Buddhist temples are still frequented, and altars with Buddhist or Taoist gods are often seen in Chinese restaurants and other businesses.

Family and Community

For thousands of years in China, the family unit has been the social system upon which the culture is organized. In Chinese society, three of the five traditional relationships (father and son, husband and wife, and elder brother and younger brother) are family relationships, and the other two can be conceived in terms of the family (ruler and subject and friend and friend). Religion has been an integral part of the family through the practice of ancestor worship, with its elaborate funeral rites, mourning observances, and continuing sacrifices to the spirit of the deceased. As indicated in the section on Confucianism, rules governing family life were very explicit. If, for example, a son did not fulfill the duties of filial piety as indicated in the prevailing mores of the time, he was disowned.

As in other traditional societies, marriage has been the institution concerned with the production and nurturing of children. Reinforced by Confucianism in Chinese culture, marriage is also a requirement for carrying on the family lineage, supporting the elderly, and maintaining the connection with family ancestors. Originally, couples did not marry for love; in fact, romantic love was frowned upon. Couples married for functional reasons: taking care of parents, improving the position of the family, and bringing sons into the world. Marriages were arranged by parents to ensure that they were appropriate. The son and his wife were required to live with his parents; they owed absolute obedience to them and had no independent property rights. Wives were subservient to their husbands and mothers-in-law. If a wife could not produce a son, her husband was allowed to have a son from a concubine. If a wife was widowed, she was not permitted to remarry.

By living according to Confucian ideals, family members expected to experience self-respect, nurturance, and enrichment through the sincere, kind, and fair honoring of their roles. They also expected to experience affection as they raised their children and came together for family and communal celebrations. In reality, however, people are people, and as in any other culture, henpecking of husbands, gossiping among older women regarding their daughters-in-law, spoiling of children, infidelity, and abusive behavior occurred frequently.

The community or village was simply an extension of the family. As in any community, people banded together for friendship, identity, mutual aid, recreation, and protection against natural disasters and those of human origin. People honored many cultural and family rituals and observances, as well as building temples for prayer, offices for conducting business, and places for dining and recreation. Behavior and social norms were ruled by imperial or governmental dictates, etiquette, and traditions. Individuals had to conform not only to rigid family norms but to communal norms as well (Hsu, 1971).

According to the Confucian order of prestige, the four main classes of Chinese society were scholars, farmers, workers (artisans and laborers), and merchants. Nobility, clergy, and military were not even mentioned as classes because they were not part of the mainstream and were only present for functional purposes. In theory, any man could aspire to leave his village and be a scholarly official by passing a series of examinations (Eberhard, 1971). Thus, in the Confucian scale of values, the ideal was to be an educated, successful, scholarly government official. Farmers and workers were seen as honest people who contributed to the welfare of society, while businesspeople were seen as social parasites who did nothing but earn a living from the labor of others.

Differences Among Chinese

Family therapists must be aware of the fact that just as Asian Americans do not form one homogeneous group, neither do the Chinese living in America. According to Uba and Sue (1991), the differences are based on numerous variables, including

- Place of origin in China
- Country from which they emigrated
- Circumstances of their immigration
- Time period of their immigration
- Generation and age
- Degree of assimilation
- Educational level
- Socioeconomic status
- Occupational skills
- Religious beliefs
- Support system

These variables influence the way the needs of groups within the Chinese American population are defined and assessed. For example, there are major differences, including language, between Chinese from Shanghai in northern China and those from Kwantung in the south. The needs of the twenty thousand Chinese forced to leave Vietnam in the 1970s, many with little or nothing but their lives, are probably far different from those of immigrants with resources who planned to leave Hong Kong before the Communist takeover in 1997. The needs of the Chinese immigrants of my parents' generation would not be the same as those of the tens of thousands of Chinese students from Hong Kong and Taiwan who changed their immigration status to remain in this country.

These differences within the Chinese American population also influence the types of treatment issues that are brought to therapy.

Some families bring with them concerns related to resettlement or cultural adjustment. Others have intergenerational issues, family violence, or marital conflict. Still others have severe psychopathology, including addictive behaviors. Interventions range from providing or assisting in the acquisition of education, training, services, and resources to providing individual, family, and group therapy.

How treatment interventions are addressed is dependent on the unique characteristics of those being served. Therapists might work quite differently with recent immigrants with little or no education than they would with highly educated third- or fourth-generation individuals. For the former, they might use folk medicines, acupuncture, or stress-reducing exercises, whereas better intervention choices for the latter might be Emotionally Focused Therapy, brief treatment with Solution Focused Therapy, or individual psychotherapy.

Traditional Chinese Attitudes Toward Mental Health

An ethnic group's cultural practices, medical beliefs, and customs play a significant role in the group's concept of normality and tolerance for deviant behavior, as well as in its attitudes toward accepting helpful resources (Lee, 1982). Different ethnic groups define problems, seek solutions to them, and use therapists differently. According to McGoldrick (1982), ethnic groups differ in (1) their experience of mental illness or health, (2) how symptoms are recognized and named, (3) how psychological insecurities and pain are communicated, (4) their understanding of the nature of their problem, (5) their viewpoint toward helpers, and (6) what they envision or want in treatment. Consequently, these issues must be taken into consideration if a therapist is to make an accurate assessment and develop an effective treatment plan.

The scientific approach to understanding mental illness began in the 1800s. Since that time, through the disciplines of psychiatry, psychology, and social work, numerous theories and practice models related to mental illness as well as to intrapersonal, interpersonal, and family conflict have been established. In American culture, mental illness and psychological pain are recognized as being normal, and seeking help for them is viewed as not much different from finding assistance for a physical ailment.

In recent years, acceptance and understanding of personal and interpersonal problems have been supported by "pop psychology" and self-help groups such as Alcoholics Anonymous. Hundreds of books, some of which have become national best-sellers, have been published to help with every psychological and interpersonal problem imaginable. Large followings have been established by charismatic personalities and "pop gurus" such as Laura Schlessinger, John Gray, Barbara D'Anglus, Scott Peck, John Bradshaw, and Anthony Robbins. In today's cultural climate, it has become fashionable to have and talk about personal problems.

Unlike Western culture, however, traditional Chinese culture does not view mental illness or personal or family problems from a scientific or psychological perspective. Instead, Chinese believe that mental illness is caused by spiritual unrest, hereditary weakness, metaphysical factors such as fate or an imbalance between yin and yang, or weakness of character (Lee, 1982; Browne and Broderick, 1994). Interpersonal problems and the various unconscious defense and coping mechanisms used to contend with them are not considered a consequence of psychological insecurities resulting from negative childhood experiences, but rather as a weakness of character passed on from one generation to the next. Family conflicts are not seen as a struggle for differentiation, independence, or self-esteem, but rather as a manifestation of shameful, disrespectful, and unethical conduct on the part of those involved. Parents may not be demonstrating kindness, children filial piety, or siblings respect toward one another. Marital conflicts exist not as a result of misunderstanding each other's feelings, having poor communication skills, or desiring equality. Instead they are a consequence of spouses not honoring their prescribed roles.

There is no such thing as pop psychology in Chinese culture. Books are not written to help individuals understand their relationships, feelings, behaviors, or motives. Self-help groups are not established to provide insight, encouragement, or emotional support. The search for support and understanding and the expression of angry or frustrating feelings happen within the natural confines of the family or community, among family members, friends, or community leaders. Changes or interventions are sought through prayer, gift offerings to the gods, or attempts to change the flow of energy. I had a friend, for example, who was beset by a number of personal problems. He believed that his personal problems were related to the way his home was arranged and the negative way in which energy flowed through it. He built a new wall to redirect that energy. His beliefs, and his actions based on them, caused his problems to dissipate.

Psychosomatic Symptoms

Acceptance of psychosomatic medicine has been a part of Chinese culture. Traditionally, every organ has psychological meaning or symbolic functions. The heart is considered to be the seat of intellect; the lungs are the seat of righteousness; the gall bladder is symbolic of bravery; while kidneys produce ingenuity and power (Williams, 1976). Consequently, an exploration of somatic complaints needs to be part of a family therapist's assessment of the problems of his or her Chinese clients.

As my mother grew older, she appeared to be plagued with an increasing number of physical ailments: headaches, back and stomach pains, and an inability to move various joints. One day, my brothers Chester, Douglas, and I watched her coming out of the kitchen in the back area of our grocery store. She was dragging one leg and had her right hand on her forehead as she complained of having a severe headache. It looked so contrived that it seemed comical, instead of eliciting feelings of sympathy. We looked at each other, thinking that she was a hypochondriac. Later, I learned that to the Chinese, somatization is a valid way of expressing inner conflicts and that physical, rather than psychological, complaints are an acceptable way to obtain attention. In the case of my mother, we learned from her physician that she was suffering from migraine headaches and arthritis. Chinese find it embarrassing to express feelings of rejection, loneliness, and sadness but, being especially concerned with the body and its function, they find it easy to somatize (Lee, 1982).

Suicide

Another important factor to understand when working with Chinese is that suicide is an acceptable way to save face and resolve problems. The pressure to avert shame, and particularly shame brought on the family, often drives individuals to kill themselves. This is reflected, in part, by the fact that the suicide rate among Chinese in the United States is far greater than it is among Caucasians.

Elderly Chinese immigrants are especially vulnerable to committing suicide. A study by Yu (1986) shows their suicide rate as almost three times higher than the rate for U.S.-born older Chinese Americans. The major contributing factor to this problem is depression that is caused in part by the stresses associated with immigration, the language barrier, acculturation problems, poverty, illness, and social isolation.

Understanding Chinese American Families from a Chinese Perspective

There are major differences between Chinese and American cultures. The values, beliefs, and customs in Chinese culture, as indicated in the preceding section, are intricately interwoven with Confucianism, Taoism, and Buddhism. On the other hand, American values, beliefs, and customs are interwoven with Judeo-Christian religious beliefs. Equally important, if not more so, American culture is heavily influenced by its political system, with its emphasis on equal rights and equal opportunity, and its economic system, with its emphasis on science, technology, consumerism, and improving the quality of life. As mental health professionals, we need to minimize and prevent cultural biases and shortsightedness by fostering a culturally sensitive practice in helping Chinese American clients and their families (Tseng and Hsu, 1991). Understanding these differences, as discussed briefly in the following sections, may help to accomplish this goal.

Patterns of Relationship

Cultural patterns of relationship, which vary enormously among societies, influence or dictate position of authority, definition of roles, and primary alliances, as well as how and with whom members can communicate. The established patterns are based on tradition, values, norms, and customs; however, as a result of changes from both inside and outside the culture, they do change over time. Through the influence of capitalism, science, and technology, for example, the conventional means of relating to others in China are being altered. Nevertheless, the manner in which Americans relate tends to be based on equality, independence, and negotiation, while Chinese relationships are based on structure, conformity, and custom.

Egalitarian Versus Hierarchical Patterns. The foundation of American society is egalitarian, with the emphasis on political and social equality for all. This perspective is present in family life as well: spouses want equality and reciprocity in defining their roles, determining the nature of their relationships, negotiating differences, and fulfilling personal goals and aspirations. In many instances, children are treated as peers by their parents, being given equal say in what they do and how they conduct their lives. For example, they can decide on the clothes they wish to wear, the people with whom they associate, and the college they wish to attend. The government often supports the rights of children against their parents, as when adolescents are allowed to have an abortion without their parents' permission.

Chinese society, on the other hand, is hierarchical, with each person knowing her or his roles and responsibilities in the home, community, and state. As indicated previously, the wife is subordinate to her husband, younger children to older children, girls to boys, and wives to their mothers-in-law. The emphasis in the culture is on obedience, not negotiation. In discussions of differences between those in the superior and subordinate roles, the final decision is in the hands of the person in a higher position. To be disobedient is to be disloyal and disrespectful and to bring shame.

The strict adherence to hierarchy and role expectations can, however, create problems in Chinese American families. Being put into a secondary position in relation to their brothers, for example, frequently creates resentment in girls, who feel less loved and unimportant. This resentment can result in oppositional behavior, drug abuse, and dysfunctional relationships. Many wives, believing that they have no personal rights or alternatives, will remain in abusive and exploitative relationships. As a result, they may become depressed or physically ill. Finally, it is not uncommon for men to acquiesce to an unwanted arranged marriage out of obligation to the family. Such marriages often lead to a lifetime of dejection, disappointment, and unhappiness.

Individual Versus Family Values.   One of the major building blocks in American culture is the value placed on individual growth, development, and achievement. Adults are expected to be autonomous and self-sufficient, live independently, and attain personal success. Child-rearing practices are based on this value; therefore, parents are required to provide a loving and supportive environment for their children that fosters self-esteem, independence, and personal accomplishments. Adolescent rebellion is viewed as being part of the normal developmental process leading to healthy adulthood. It is considered normal for adolescents to have an identity crisis, which helps to foster autonomy, self-reliance, and emancipation. Parents are expected to respect the individual rights of their children. This is expressed, in part, by negotiating differences they may have with them. Parents who do not following this practice are often criticized as being rigid, controlling, and insensitive. In marriage, the emphasis remains on maintaining autonomy, finding personal satisfaction, and fostering individual growth.

The emphasis in Chinese culture is not on the individual but on the integrity of the family. The needs of the individual are subordinate to those of the family. Personal satisfaction is achieved through honoring one's roles, meeting obligations, and living a harmonious family life. Adults are expected to care for both their children and their extended family. Parents are expected to provide a disciplined environment in which children are taught to be diligent in their studies, respectful, compliant, and interdependent. Children are expected to perform exceptionally well in school, in addition to helping with household chores and child-rearing responsibilities.

Unfortunately, many children do not have the intellectual capacity or desire to do well in school. Those who do not meet their parents' expectations may feel fearful, anxious, and inadequate. Many children spend an inordinate amount of time studying and become socially delayed, with no time to develop friendships and social skills. Furthermore, because of the emphasis on mature behavior, children are often ushered into adulthood and adult responsibilities too quickly, resulting in a loss of the childhood experiences that are so important for adult development.

Individuality Versus Lineage. Individuality, or taking pride in one's own success, one's own unique and distinct character, is an attribute highly regarded in American society. The "rugged individual" is admired for having a strong character, the ability to stand alone, and the will to overcome any adversity to achieve success. The emphasis on individuality begins in childhood, when children are encouraged to take pride in who they are and what they have accomplished. In fact, a child's achievements are often seen as being independent of the encouragement and support given to them by their parents.

Family connections are more important in Chinese society than individuality. Chinese people perceive themselves as standing not alone, but in relationship to their current families and to their ancestors. The successes or failures of individuals and families were often attributed to their ancestors. In this way, ancestor worship formalized the connection between the living and their predecessors. Chinese families also think that it is important to have sons to carry on their lineage and name, and that their children's behavior today either positively or negatively influences the behavior of future generations.

In the United States, Chinese parents' heavy emphasis on retaining their Chinese heritage and connection with the past, coupled with their rigid rules and expectations, may lead to the opposite of what they desire. Their children often manifest a "reaction formation" and rebel against their cultural heritage by criticizing their parents' values and belief systems, denying their ancestry, and identifying themselves as American or Asian American and marrying interethnically. In the latter case, parents sometimes disown their children, which can create even more problems.

Cultural Perspectives

Americans living in a highly capitalistic society and Chinese in an agrarian one would naturally have different worldviews. Those views, among other things, govern and influence the nature of relationships, values, mores, and what is and is not meaningful with regard to living a satisfying lifestyle. To flourish and be successful, Chinese immigrants must somehow find harmony between the worldview to which they are accustomed and the worldview of their adopted country. This is no easy task given the wide schism between the two perspectives.

Modern Versus Traditional Worldviews. American culture is modern and relatively young, dating back only a few hundred years, and Americans adhere to only a few traditions. With the heavy influence of science, technology, consumerism, and the high cost of living, Americans are faced with an accelerated rate of change in their relationships to other people, things, places, and organizations, and to ideals, information, and values. They also must cope with increasing numbers of situations, events, and dilemmas that are completely new. Finally, they have too much choice in their daily lives. In short, due to modernization, a large number of Americans appear to be overextended, faced with numerous changes and decisions that are driven by the forces in their environment, and looking to the future to find peace.

In Chinese culture, on the other hand, many ancient traditions and rituals are observed. These traditions and rituals are considered to consist of more than exterior correctness or adherence to a particular custom or belief; they are an outward expression of the love and obligation by which one is bound to others. Although the culture is beginning to change as China becomes more industrialized, the emphasis in Chinese society has always been on revering the past while maintaining sameness and seeking stability and tranquillity in the present.

Immigrant parents may be grounded in their identity and traditions, but their first-generation children or their children's children are often confused about themselves. They are pulled in one direction by parents who wish them to adhere to Chinese traditions and customs that are often diametrically opposed to the dominant culture. On the other hand, they are pulled toward assimilation by the dominant culture, which emphasizes change, equality, and materialism. The children may feel marginal, or not fully belonging to either worldview, yet they do not have the insight, support, or guidance to integrate the two views. Some will address their confusion by identifying themselves as Asian Americans. Depending on how they internalize this identity, it can help them to integrate their Chinese and American heritages or foster denial of both of them. Others will deny their Chinese heritage altogether and identify themselves as Americans. The extreme position is reflected when Chinese names are Anglicized or when Chinese undergo operations on their eyes to remove their Asian look.

Materialistic Versus Altruistic Values.   The United States is a consumer-driven society with one of the highest standards of living in the world. The American dream is to live a middle-class lifestyle, which is reflected in part by owning a home furnished with modern appliances and conveniences, driving a nice automobile, and wearing fashionable clothes. Often an individual's self-esteem, significance, or dignity is based on these outward appearances and what he or she has acquired. This has led to the tendency of many Americans to become more concerned with material goods than with spiritual values such as altruism.

In Chinese society, greater value, honor, and prestige are placed on altruism than on materialism. According to Confucian ethics, altruism, or the unselfish concern for the welfare of others, is one of the highest virtues one can possess. Without it, a person's life is meaningless. My father-in-law possesses this virtue, and even though he worked in a laundry and did not acquire much financial success, he is loved, respected, and honored by his family, his friends, and members of his community.

Self-Perceptions

No matter what their culture, people wish to feel personal self-esteem or pride in who they are and what they have accomplished. How this occurs, of course, varies among societies and is based on each society's values, norms, and worldview. The American and Chinese cultures operate from different paradigms with regard to this issue.

Self-Esteem Versus Virtue.   In American society, personal esteem is based on self-esteem or how one feels toward oneself. Even though it will fluctuate throughout their life, people's sense of self-esteem is seen as primarily influenced by their home environment and the degree to which it was loving, understanding, supportive, and fair. Positive self-esteem is evidenced, in part, by recognizing and accepting one's strengths as well as weaknesses, making decisions that enhance one's personal and spiritual growth, and participating in relationships that are mutually enriching. People with poor self-esteem feel insecure and fearful and may involve themselves in relationships that are detrimental to their well-being. Such individuals often require therapy to assist them in gaining or regaining a positive view of themselves.

Personal esteem in Chinese culture is not based on self-esteem but rather on virtue. Confucius believed that human nature was good and that every person should strive to manifest that goodness by living a virtuous life. Such a life included honoring one's roles; demonstrating love, compassion, and humility; and perpetuating justice. Living a virtuous life brought respect both to individuals and to their families and ancestors. Living a life without integrity or virtue brought shame to individuals, their families, and their ancestors.

Guilt Versus Shame.   American morality, being heavily influenced by Judeo-Christian beliefs, is regulated by guilt, the feeling experienced when individuals go against their moral code. Guilt reflects on people's integrity and reminds them that they are not perfect. It therefore allows them to understand and accept others' fallibility. It also gives them the opportunity to redirect their life; fosters feelings of sadness, empathy, and compassion; and invites forgiveness. In addition, guilt provides individuals with the opportunity to ask others for help and the chance to experience courage by apologizing for any injuries they may have caused.

Chinese society, as indicated previously, is highly structured and governed by countless rules regulating behavior. Its morality, therefore, is regulated by shame rather than guilt. Shame is the negative emotion associated with misbehaving or going contrary to cultural codes of conduct. Normal shame, the everyday embarrassments and humiliations that we feel for ourselves and others, arises from several sources: rejection, failure, and impropriety. It typically includes the feeling of having broken the law. As with guilt, shame allows individuals to feel remorseful and to correct their inappropriate behavior, apologize to those they have insulted, or rectify the harm they have caused. However, unlike guilt, which only reflects on the misconduct of the individuals involved, shame in Chinese society reflects on both individuals and their families and ancestors.

Many Chinese immigrant parents feel inappropriate shame. They may be extremely poor or lack the educational skills and resources to make an adequate adjustment to their adopted country. They may be poor amid a society of plenty. They then may take responsibility for the circumstances in which they are living and blame themselves for making wrong decisions, planning poorly, or being unable to care for their families. To make matters worse, children will frequently blame their parents for their unhappy circumstances, leading them to participate in delinquent or criminal behavior, join gangs, or take drugs. Unable to change their circumstances, the parents cannot diminish the tremendous shame they experience.

Types of Expression

Americans and Chinese differ in the manner in which they express themselves, the former relying on honesty and the right of free speech and the latter on propriety, formality, and sensitivity. Chinese are concerned about respecting the unique and inalienable value of others as much as they respect their own. It is therefore important to them to speak in a way that avoids bringing shame or disrespect on themselves or others.

Direct Versus Indirect Communication.   Americans place a high value on being explicit, assertive, and direct in their conversations. This behavior is viewed as openness and honesty, which provides the foundation for building a relationship based on genuineness and sincerity. Courses are given and numerous books written to help individuals conduct themselves in this manner.

Among Chinese, however, being assertive and direct is viewed as inappropriate behavior because it might cause others to feel shame or lose face. They will go to great lengths to see that this does not happen and prefer to speak indirectly.

I recall, for example, an incident when Po Po (my wife Rosie's mother) was talking about how people today simply discard the elderly by putting them in nursing homes; she implied by her tone that she wondered if we were going to do that with her. I asked her if she was thinking that we would do such a thing. She said no, but the message in her indirect expression was clear.

Expression of Feelings Versus Control of Feelings.   American society has a strong emphasis on awareness, understanding, and the free expression of feelings. More often than not, how we behave is based on unconscious feelings rather than on what we think. Becoming aware of our feelings can lead us to a better understanding of ourselves and our relationships with others.

Chinese, however, do not believe in being aware of their feelings or verbally expressing them. In fact, they believe that controlling one's strong feelings is necessary for maintaining mental health (Lum, 1982). Instead of focusing on affect, the Chinese focus on maintaining a quiet reserve and appropriate conduct. This does not mean that they are not playful, spontaneous, and demonstrative. They can be, but only in the appropriate circumstances.

This chapter addressed the importance for therapists of being culturally sensitive to and aware of the differences between American and Chinese cultures. Without such recognition, therapists will be very limited in their ability to help Chinese American families that need assistance. A knowledge of cultural issues and distinctions is foundational to understanding how to best treat Chinese and Chinese American clients and their families. Chapter Three describes Chinese American Family Therapy, which is based on many of the ideas and concepts regarding Chinese culture just presented.

From whos perspectives?

Boundary issue?

Chapter Three

A Chinese Model for Family Therapy

Chinese American Family Therapy (CAFT) is an eclectic, multi-dimensional, comprehensive family therapy model in which family integration theory, general systems theory, and case management act as foundational theories, combined with crisis intervention and social learning theory. Other models such as Structural Family Therapy, Strategic Therapy, and Planned Short-Term Treatment may be used in conjunction with CAFT as needed.

This model respects and values both Chinese and Western cultures, not idealizing either but recognizing that both have strengths and advantages as well as weaknesses and shortcomings. CAFT is also a model that adds to and allows therapists to build upon their current body of knowledge and practice skills. This chapter describes CAFT's theoretical framework and its principles of practice and interventions in regard to the role of therapists and treatment procedures.

CAFT is a brief, prescriptive, and problem-centered approach designed for Chinese American families seeking assistance from social service, child welfare, mental health, and family counseling agencies. The problems brought to these agencies often result from our clients' inability to maintain or achieve family integration because of a crisis, lack of support or resources to live physically healthy and emotionally satisfying lives, and family conflicts. The model addresses these issues in an effective and sensitive manner.

The CAFT model uses the concept of family integration as the cornerstone of its conceptual framework and underpins it with ethical principles founded on Confucian humanitarianism. *Family integration* is defined as the state of being in a harmonious relationship with one's family by learning to live ethically with family members. For Chinese Americans to live a harmonious life, they must relate to their family within the context of Chinese American culture. The task of individual family members, therefore, is to understand their cultural context and then live accordingly. In many instances, however, problems arise because of the inability of family members to negotiate or assimilate cultural differences. CAFT's goal is to help such families resolve those as well as other problems that prevent family integration and to help family members to live ethically in harmonious relationship to one another. This is accomplished by using clinical interventions and techniques based on the theories and models incorporated in CAFT, CAFT's own principles of practice, and other models that can be used in conjunction with it.

Now let us take a more detailed look at general systems theory, the first of the five frameworks underpinning CAFT. This theory describes the way Chinese families function as interdependent systems and provides a foundation upon which clinical interventions are based.

General Systems Theory

The Chinese family is a system composed of interrelated and interdependent parts. Because the whole is greater than the sum of its parts, the interrelationship of the units gives rise to new qualities that are a function of that interrelationship. In addition, change in one part of the system affects the system as a whole and all of its parts (Von Bertalanffy, 1968).

Families are living and open systems, influencing and being influenced by the environments in which they live. They are governed, in part, by boundaries or sets of invisible rules and regulations that govern the flow of energy: ideas, information, friendships, resources, and so on. Permeable boundaries allow energy and information to be imported from the environments for maintenance and survival while rigid ones close off family systems, fostering entropy, randomness, or dysfunction.

Families are self-regulating in their sense of coherence, order, and inner character. Through various feedback processes, they seek to maintain a homeostatic balance to ensure their integrity. Homeostasis is not a static state, but a moving state with a range of stability within which the system moves (Miller, 1975). This is important because in order to grow and survive, families must learn to adapt to changes from both within and without. Key to this process of adaptation is the ability of families to receive, process, store, and make use of information (Hartman and Laird, 1983).

Implications for Treatment

Several important principles for working with Chinese families can be drawn from general systems theory. Whenever possible, it is important for therapists to see the family rather than the individual. This provides them with a more authentic picture of the dynamics, issues, and problems of those being treated, because interactional patterns can be observed firsthand. It also gives them more alternatives for intervening and for assessing the ramifications of the interventions on the family system as a whole. Furthermore, given the hierarchical nature of Chinese families, obtaining the support of those in the dominant position of authority maximizes the possibilities for change.

It is not important to promote big changes that will create significant disruption of the family's homeostatic balance. In fact, this might lead to major resistance. A change in one member of the family, whether it is small or major, can lead to significant changes in the entire system, so although it is preferable to see all the members of a family in treatment, it is not always necessary.

Given the rigid boundary keeping of traditional Chinese families, it is important to work toward making boundaries more permeable. Without permeability, members of the family cannot obtain, understand, or use the information and resources required to make appropriate changes and adaptations. Furthermore, as I have indicated, closed or rigid systems that are in need of adaptation tend to foster negative energy flow and dysfunction.

As therapists, we must acknowledge and respect the rules and regulations governing the maintenance of homeostatic balance in the families with which we are working. However, this does not stop us from challenging the rules or offering new information, especially if these alternatives help in resolving the dysfunction that has been brought to treatment. For example, the primary role of a father who is also abusive should be respected and supported, and his inappropriate conduct should be challenged and alternatives offered without his children being present.

One of our major roles as therapists working with traditional Chinese families must be that of mediator. We must provide Chinese families with a bridge between their culture and the culture of their adopted country. We must help families to discern which aspects of their culture are important to keep and maintain in order to ensure the integrity of the family. We must also convey to families that adaptation and acculturation are normal and necessary for growth and survival.

In addition to helping Chinese families understand the importance of adaptation and acculturation, we need to assist many of them in acquiring the necessary resources and services to succeed in this country. The case management model described in the next section provides us with a conceptual framework that permits us to achieve this task in a planned, orderly, and efficient manner.

Case Management

Case management has reemerged over the past two decades as a service intervention model because of the many changes that have affected the delivery of health and human services. More specifically, some of the events influencing its recent reemergence have been the impact of deinstitutionalization on human service delivery, decentralization of community services, the presence within communities of client populations with significant problems of social functioning, recognition of the crucial roles of social support and social networks in the social functioning of individuals, fragmentation of human services, and the growing concern with the cost-effectiveness of human services (Moxley, 1989).

According to Rubin (1992, p. 5), case management is "an approach to service delivery that attempts to ensure that clients with complex, multiple problems and disabilities receive all the services that they need in a timely and appropriate fashion." This approach has been applied to several problem areas including alcohol and drug abuse, chronic mental illness, the social service needs of the elderly, AIDS, juvenile delinquency, and child abuse and neglect. No matter what the issue, however, our primary role as case managers is that of caseworkers whose responsibilities include

- Assessing the needs of clients
- Developing a plan of action to meet those needs
- Assisting clients in implementing the service plan
- Monitoring that service plan
- Reassessing and, if necessary, working to change what has been planned
- Evaluating whether or not the service plan was successful

Secondary roles include being a broker, advocate, educator, counselor, consultant, or mediator.

The underpinning of case management is ecological theory, which recognizes that family life is an evolutionary process that is in constant motion, with family systems continuing to influence and be influenced by the environments within which they are interacting. It also recognizes the interconnectedness and interdependency among individuals, their families, and their environments. Problems are seen as being related to the ability or inability of families to obtain the necessary resources to address and adapt to the stressors and deficits they experience in their environments.

The ecological concept of "goodness of fit" indicates a functional adaptive process with a balanced flow of positive energy between families and their environments. Thus, problems are viewed as inappropriate adaptive strategies, dysfunctional transactions between systems, or deficits in the environment, rather than as deficiencies in individuals. Deficits that create stress and a negative flow of energy away from individuals and families can include lack of adequate housing, unsafe neighborhoods, unemployment, discrimination, and unavailable or unassessable mental health, child welfare, or family services (Libassi, 1992).

The heart of case management is a focus on empowering clients. According to Gibson (1993), "Empowerment theory is based on the assumption that the capacity of people to improve their lives is determined by their ability to control their environment, connect with needed resources, negotiate problematic situations, and change existing social situations that limit human functioning" (p. 389). By working to empower people, we highlight our values of believing in the uniqueness and inherent dignity of the individual and believing in client self-determination. Doing things for clients puts them in an inferior position, encourages dependency, ignores their abilities and strengths, and prevents personal growth. The emphasis in case management is, therefore, on working collaboratively rather than dictatorially with clients, emphasizing strengths rather than weaknesses, and providing support rather than fostering reliance.

As case managers, we should not be doing for our clients; we should be working with them to acquire the skills, support, and resources to manage their lives in a meaningful and life-enhancing manner.

Implications for Treatment

The multiple needs of many Chinese immigrants are well known and include such things as housing, income, employment, job training, English language skills, medical and child care, and transportation. Some immigrants arrive already depleted of resources and therefore are subject to crisis, loss of physical health, depression, and exploitation by unscrupulous employers; they may live in isolation, substandard housing conditions, or dangerous neighborhoods. Even worse, they are subject to the loss of respect and dignity. In short, there is no goodness of fit between many Chinese immigrant families and their adopted country, particularly those on the lower end of the socioeconomic scale. Case management can be extremely useful for such families.

Case management's concrete, pragmatic, and problem- and task-centered approach to helping clients is ideally suited to what Chinese families expect from social, child welfare, and mental health services. The model's strength of perspective, emphasis on empowerment, and assessment that focuses on a lack of resources rather than on individual deficiencies serves to help our clients retain their sense of self-respect and integrity in the face of having to humble themselves by being forced to rely on outsiders for assistance. Furthermore, the collaborative relationship established in treatment and the principle of using the client's life experience to find solutions to problems serve to reinforce the client's sense of intelligence, expertness, and competency.

The coordination and multiplicity of services offered by case management helps our clients to reduce the feeling of being overwhelmed and fragmented that they often experience in the face of immense adversity. The emphasis on helping clients to obtain resources such as language skills, adequate housing, or legal assistance begins to reverse the negative energy flow away from the family and thereby facilitates an effective adaptation to the family's environment. Finally, helping clients to recognize that one change in their situation can have major positive ramifications in many areas of their life gives them hope for the future. Finding a satisfactory job for one member of the family, for example, can provide financial stability, adequate housing, and an opportunity for upward mobility.

The many roles, functions, and tasks we can use as case managers allow our clients to receive a variety of services from one person. In our role of broker, for example, we can link clients to a spectrum of services and resources. As counselors, we can use therapeutic interventions to assist families in resolving interpersonal conflicts; as educators, we can provide necessary information in a number of important areas, such as how to obtain citizenship, fill out a job application, or receive public assistance. Finally, as advocates, we can inform clients of their legal rights or provide agency support in obtaining programs and services to which they are entitled.

Crisis Intervention

Crisis intervention theory postulates that everyone encounters and lives with stressful situations or events in his or her daily life. These situations may include being late for an appointment, being involved in a minor car accident, or performing poorly on an examination. They may also include transitional conditions such as adjusting to a new marriage, experiencing a job transfer, or beginning college. Finally, they may include chronic situations such as constant pressure to perform on the job, adjustment to a major disability, or recovery from an addiction. The ability to handle these stressors effectively is based on the resources that are brought to them, which include intellectual functioning, emotional maturity, financial means, and the support of family and friends. Those who lack resources, such as low-income, unskilled, and uneducated Chinese immigrants, are generally more vulnerable or more predisposed to crisis.

A crisis is a temporary state in which individuals or families do not have the resources to cope effectively with the stress or trauma they are encountering. This results in their feeling distraught and overwhelmed cognitively, affectively, and behaviorally. In the acute phase of a crisis, individuals normally feel helpless, depressed, and hopeless and are unable to care for themselves (Wells, 1982).

Crises may be triggered by an extremely painful event such as being raped; losing a loved one through death, divorce, or separation; or surviving a physical disaster. It is not only the event itself that creates the crisis, but also our perception of that event. Some people, for example, do not perceive being robbed, losing their home, or undergoing a divorce as a major or catastrophic event, whereas others do. Our perceptions are influenced, in part, by emotional vulnerability, experience with former crises, and what we feel is important in life (Hill, 1965).

Normally, the length of the acute phase of a crisis is six to eight weeks, after which an individual who is provided with appropriate support and understanding will begin to rise out of the depths of chaos. For example, most suicides occur during the early upswing of a crisis, when individuals have enough emotional energy to look ahead, see no positive future, and feel the full impact of hopelessness. It is not a feeling of bravery, as many people believe, that allows individuals to kill themselves, but despair. The upswing of cognitive, affective, and behavioral abilities continues until the individuals reach either a lower level than they functioned at before the crisis, the same level, or a higher level. The level they arrive and stay at is based on several variables, including the emotional support they receive, their level of maturity, and their philosophical, religious, or cultural outlook toward life.

Implications for Treatment

Chinese families, like other clients, are often seen in treatment because of a crisis. The objective of crisis intervention therapy is to assist them in returning to the same level as their functioning before the crisis. This is accomplished through following six guiding principles:

1.   We provide a supportive and understanding therapeutic atmosphere, especially in light of the fact that many Chinese clients feel embarrassed at having to be in treatment in the first place. This is accomplished, in part, by conveying active empathy and a genuine concern regarding their well-being.

2.   We move to normalize our clients' thoughts, feelings, and behaviors. Many Chinese feel ashamed or believe that something

is wrong with them because they are contemplating suicide or are not available to others who may also be in pain. They may think that they are irresponsible because they neglect normal daily responsibilities or do not go to work. We explain to such individuals that in their current circumstances they should not feel disgraced or dishonored and that what they are thinking and experiencing and the way they are behaving is appropriate. We then go on to explain the stages of crisis and what they can expect during the following several weeks. We say that they will begin to feel better naturally and will take control of their lives again. These first two procedures are repeated continuously throughout treatment.

3.   We work toward helping our clients identify or find support for the emotional turmoil they are experiencing. Preferably, support systems within their own family, friendships, and social networks are used. These may include parents, close friends, or a support group within their church. This is often very difficult because many Chinese believe that it is shameful and a sign of weak character to disclose their personal problems to friends or other family members. In such cases, we assist these clients in finding support elsewhere.

4.   We stay focused in the present, addressing the issues that are immediately at hand. If necessary, we help clients and their families find solutions to the issues that have been raised during the crisis. This might include obtaining medical leave from their work or finding child care.

5.   We explore with clients the impact the crisis might be having, or will have, on their life, making sure not to use platitudes like "It was fate" or to give lengthy discourses on how they can grow and learn from what has happened.

6.   We terminate therapy by having the clients summarize their experience with us and tell us what they plan to do in the near future. This direct and concrete approach is useful to Chinese, who expect treatment to be practical and sensible. Before saying farewell, clients are told that they are welcome to return or give us a telephone call if they have any further questions.

Social Learning Theory

A major postulate of social learning theory is that all behavior is learned and negative behavior can be unlearned. Among the basic tenets of the theory (Bandura, 1977; Rotter, 1954) are several concepts: (1) behavior is controlled by its consequences (operant conditioning) and by the operation of particular reinforcing patterns, (2) much human behavior is learned through imitation of observed models, and (3) the learning and performance of behaviors commonly are mediated by cognitive processes that include irrational beliefs, unrealistic expectations, and biases that promote negative interactions.

Operant conditioning shapes family interactions when family members provide reinforcement for some of each other's responses and punishment for other responses. This process begins with the earliest interactions among family members. Each person learns about discriminative stimuli that signal the likelihood that particular responses will elicit reinforcement or punishment from others. The internalized expectancies that each person has about the probabilities of particular outcomes under particular circumstances are important cognitions in the learning process (Wells, 1982).

In social learning theory, the concept of reciprocity is useful in explaining how behavior is learned. A common example of the reciprocal nature of the reinforcement process in family interactions occurs when one family member complies with another in order to terminate the other's aversive behavior. Thus, if a father criticizes his daughter for not paying attention to him when he finds her on the telephone and she turns her attention to him in order to stop his criticism, she receives positive reinforcement for shifting her attention to him. In turn, he receives positive reinforcement for criticizing her. She may pay more attention to him than to her individual interests in the future because that behavior effectively terminates unpleasant stimulation (criticizing), whereas he may be more likely to criticize her in the future because this apparently elicits desirable consequences (her attention). This interactional dynamic is very powerful as a result of the highly interdependent nature of the family members' reinforcement contingencies.

Implications for Treatment

The following four axioms of social learning theory can assist us in helping Chinese families and individuals to resolve the problems they bring to treatment. First, learning takes place most efficiently when objectives and goals are clearly and concretely identified by both the client and the therapist. Second, change takes place most easily in explicitly defined linear phases or steps. Third, complex learning takes place through modeling or observing others. Finally, change takes place best through actually experiencing and reinforcing new behavior. Based on these precepts, it is important for us to

1. Help clients establish distinct objectives and goals
2. Establish a clearly defined treatment plan that defines the necessary steps to be taken
3. Model appropriate behavior
4. Foster change through actions such as creating enactments in or giving homework assignments for outside sessions, rather than just through discussions

Social learning theory helps to explain how behavior is learned and reinforced. It can therefore be used to explain how integrity and family integration, which are achieved by conducting one's life based on Confucian ethics, are or are not learned in the family. *Positive reciprocal interactions* foster movement toward integrity while *negative reciprocal interactions* encourage movement away from integrity and family integration. If parents model and teach their children the Confucian principles of fairness, loyalty, and honesty, they will learn and internalize these attributes, behave accordingly, and move toward achieving integration. However, the opposite is also true, and if unfairness, disrespect, and harshness are modeled and taught in the family, children will learn and internalize these negative attributes, which in turn will stifle family integration. Fortunately, all behavior is learned, so negative patterns of behavior can be unlearned and replaced by positive ones. This can be accomplished in therapy through various clinical interventions.

Family integration is a new clinical idea, conceived to help explain intrapersonal and interpersonal relationships in Chinese families and to provide therapists with a model that can be used to identify and resolve problems brought to treatment. Therefore, therapists may need to explain family integration to clients and describe how it can be used to understand and resolve the issues they are facing.

Family Integration

Taoism postulates that everything in nature is relative and has an opposite, and that for us to find harmony in life, we must understand and find meaning in this duality in nature. The duality is expressed in the Taoist symbols of yin and yang; the former represents, among other things, femininity, softness, passivity, and harmony, and the latter, masculinity, hardness, aggressiveness, and chaos. If the concept of relativity is accepted, we recognize that life is neither all good nor all bad and we can grow and learn from both adversity and prosperity, difficulty and success, misfortune and good fortune.

Family integration, the central concept in CAFT, is derived from this Taoist premise. Therefore, in order for traditional Chinese American families to find emotional, psychological, and spiritual peace, they must integrate or find peace with each other and with the many cultural differences between their country of origin and their adopted one. Like all immigrant groups, they must learn to assimilate into American society to some degree. This is no easy task; it requires understanding, flexibility, and a willingness to change and adapt. Many of the cultural differences that need reconciliation were alluded to in Chapter Two. They include issues related to marriage, family loyalty, and child-rearing practices.

Unfortunately, many families are unable to reconcile the clash in cultures without serious threat to the traditional Chinese family structure. This is reflected in part by the increase in divorce, juvenile delinquency, and child abuse among Chinese, as well as by cultural problems arising from interethnic and interracial marriages.

Many problems that are surfacing in Chinese American families are rooted in these cultural conflicts. More and more women are being influenced by this country's legal system and attitude toward marriage to seek divorce, because they no longer believe that they must or should tolerate the indifference of their spouse or mistreatment by their mother-in-law. Adolescents are rebelling against their parents' overly strict rules and use of corporal punishment, joining gangs for support and identity. Parents are learning that their children have rights and that if they are mistreated or neglected, the authorities will intervene. Finally, children are going against their parents' wishes and marrying the people they love regardless of their ethnic or racial identity.

Parents want their children to succeed by obtaining an advanced degree. However, this can become a double-edged sword. On one hand, their children do achieve success, but on the other, their education often fosters movement away from traditional values and beliefs. Consequently, many second-generation Chinese Americans more readily identify with and live a lifestyle based on American rather than Chinese cultural values and beliefs. All this builds conflict in Chinese American families.

In addition to reconciling the differences between Chinese and American cultures, maintaining or achieving family integration for many Chinese Americans will require overcoming and finding meaning in the many hardships they may encounter in their adopted country. These include issues related to discrimination, unemployment or underemployment, living in poor housing conditions or dangerous neighborhoods, and social isolation. For example, Joyce, a close friend of my family, recently told me that during her first two years in this country she felt extremely depressed and alone and almost returned to Taiwan because she had no friends with whom she could talk and socialize. Fortunately, she forced herself to learn English and get involved in local civic organizations to overcome her feelings of depression and loneliness.

Achieving family integration also dictates discovering meaning and finding reconciliation in what was and is positive and negative in family and societal relationships. This requires that we learn to acknowledge the love, support, and understanding of family members, especially parents, and to forgive those who may have behaved unjustly, punitively, or disrespectfully. This does not mean continuing to subject ourselves to physical or emotional abuse, unkindness, or unfairness. In fact, self-protection may require us to have very little or even no contact with those who continue to exhibit exploitative behavior. This is especially difficult for Chinese, who have been taught throughout life to remain loyal to and involved with our families under all circumstances. However, harboring negative feelings such as resentment, envy, and entitlement keeps us attached to the past, preventing peace and full enjoyment of life in the present.

Achieving family integration also requires us to have integrity, take responsibility for misconduct, and apologize to or ask for forgiveness from those we have injured by our misbehavior. In addition, we must forgive ourselves for the harm we may have deliberately or inadvertently caused to others. We must learn from our mistakes and from the adversity under which we may have lived, applying that knowledge to avoid repetition of the errors of the past; in so doing, we develop an enhanced life that will endure in the future. Finally, family integration requires us to find meaning in our lives, giving purpose to what we are doing and hope to do.

The process of family integration is continuous, beginning at birth and continuing throughout our lifetime. As children, we have very little control over that process and rely on our parents to be responsible for providing an environment in which we can experience love, safety, and tranquility. As we grow older, we develop the cognitive ability and interpersonal skills we need to begin shifting that responsibility from our parents to ourselves. By adulthood and certainly by midlife, we should be in charge of ourselves, taking full responsibility for our decisions, actions, and behaviors.

Each time we learn something beneficial from a life event or situation, even a negative one, we develop emotionally, move further toward discovering inner peace, and are better prepared to learn and grow from the next meaningful or important challenge or circumstance we will encounter. The more this cycle is repeated, the more opportunity for integration we have and therefore the greater the possibilities for developing intimate family and personal relationships.

Finally, achieving family integration requires us to incorporate and find peace with the endless number of positive and negative changes and situations that continually influence us and our interpersonal relationships. The concept of adaptation does not necessarily imply a passive acceptance of our circumstances but can include the possibility of a highly creative response. The ability to adapt in such a manner, however, requires understanding, imagination, support, and resources. It also requires the ability to exercise good judgment, discern what is authentic, and behave in a manner that is based on conviction rather than rigidity or stubbornness.

Family integration is first learned and fostered in Chinese families when parents and other adults model respect, ethical conduct, and responsible behavior. In Chinese homes, children learn the values, norms, and traditions of Chinese culture as well as how to be supportive, compassionate, and forgiving. They also learn that moral order is maintained through good personal manners and affable interpersonal relationships. They acquire the necessary knowledge and skills that will help them to overcome and learn from adversity and prepare them to live prosperous and productive lives. Finally, it is within the family that children learn to perfect themselves and thereby ensure the stability not only of their family unit but of the community as well.

The concept of family integration can be applied universally, its path defined by the values, norms, and expectations of each culture. However, the concept is uniquely suited to Chinese culture, because a major objective of Chinese clients—based on Confucian humanitarianism, Taoist philosophy, and Buddhist spirituality—is to find *harmony* in life and with the family.

Chinese who wish to achieve a high level of family integration must aspire to meet the following cultural standards, which were described in Chapter Two:

1. Family-centeredness
2. Filial loyalty, including loyalty toward ancestors
3. Conformity to role expectations, including deference to those in positions of authority
4. Ethnocentrism, which includes respecting cultural traditions and rituals
5. Situation-centeredness, or giving priority to respecting the unique and inalienable value of both oneself and others
6. The ability to conduct oneself in a prudent and reserved manner

To satisfy these standards, people should adhere to the ethical principles prescribed by Confucius: compassion or devoted love, justice, respect, loyalty, honor, responsibility, altruism, and wisdom.

Barriers to Family Integration

Achieving family integration is not an easy task given the multitude of challenges, hardships, betrayals, and disappointments all of us will encounter in our journey through life. Some of us will have to heal from the pain and emotional scars resulting from being neglected, sexually abused, or alcohol- or drug-addicted. Others will have to overcome the pain associated with a divorce or the loss of a parent or loved one, or the humiliation of experiencing various forms of discrimination. Still others will have to negotiate the differences between two cultures or find peace with a physical or emotional disability with which they have to live. No matter what the adversity, however, it must be overcome if integration is to be realized.

The clinical issues brought to treatment by Chinese families that stifle family integration fall into one or more of the following categories:

1. Unfairness
2. Exploitation
3. Cultural camouflage
4. Unreasonable expectations
5. Parentification of children
6. Pathological shaming
7. Triangulation
8. Favoritism
9. Intergenerational cultural conflict
10. Unwillingness to compromise

These issues reflect a lack of adherence to Confucian ethics. Consequently, they prevent reconciliation of interpersonal relationships and the ability to meet cultural norms, values, and expectations.

Unfairness

The foundation upon which Confucian ethics is learned, internalized, and reinforced is based on the concept of *reciprocity* or *mutual fairness*. Confucian teachings declare that every family member is entitled to certain rights and privileges. Fathers, for example, are entitled to filial piety from their children. However, this relationship, like the other principal relationships in Chinese society, is meant to be mutual and reciprocal. Children are also entitled to be treated with patience and understanding. Husbands in arranged or traditional marriages are entitled to respectful submission from their wives, but wives are entitled to receive protection, care, and consideration from their husbands. Likewise, an eldest brother, given his position and role in the Chinese family, is entitled to receive obedience and respect from his siblings, but in return they are entitled to receive gentleness and understanding from him. For whatever reason it happens, lack of adherence to the principle of reciprocity leads to unfairness and fosters untrustworthiness, disrespect, and disloyalty.

Exploitation

The most extreme form of unfairness is exploitation, where individuals in authority use their role to manipulate, subjugate, or punish their subordinates. Such relationships are based on *form*, or rigid rules and regulations, and not *substance*, that is, essence or authenticity. Exploiters are not concerned about the integrity or well-being of others, but only about meeting their own selfish needs and desires.

Exploitation is based on a lack of integrity, egotism, and ignorance. Alcoholic fathers, for example, may treat their children with abuse and callousness and yet still expect them to express filial loyalty. Husbands may treat their wives with ridicule and indifference but still expect them to be warm and supportive. Older brothers may treat their younger siblings unjustly and disrespectfully and yet expect them to be cooperative and obedient. Such exploitation stifles harmony and fosters dissonance, reactiveness, and conflict.

Cultural Camouflage

One way that unfairness or exploitation is maintained is through the use of cultural camouflage. This defense mechanism allows individuals to hide behind something in their ethnic or racial background in order to avoid responsibility for feelings and actions or to justify rigid adherence to a particular dysfunctional belief or behavior.

This defense mechanism is often accompanied by *selective memory*, whereby individuals choose only the useful information from a concept and disregard the rest.

A Chinese father once told me that he was justified in beating his son for lying because his cultural background gave parents authority over their children, including the right to punish them for misbehaving. I reminded him that he had forgotten that his culture also required parents to be patient, kind, understanding, and forgiving.

Unreasonable Expectations

Many Chinese parents come to treatment with unreasonable expectations for their children, some of which are culturally related while others are not. Education, for example, is highly valued in Chinese culture, and many children are expected to go on to college for advanced degrees whether or not they have the ability or desire to do so. Other children, regardless of their beliefs or how they feel, are forbidden to date or marry non-Chinese, even when no Chinese are available. Still others are expected to keep quiet and not express any negative thoughts or feelings toward their parents even if they are being exploited or treated unfairly. Such inflexible expectations perpetuate angry and resentful emotions and rebellious and argumentative behaviors.

Parentification of Children

Because of a lack of access to adequate child care, many Chinese children are elevated to a position of parentified children and given the responsibility for taking care of their siblings. Many families do quite well with this arrangement, but some do not, which can normally be attributed to the following reasons:

1. Although the authority over the younger children no longer remains the responsibility of the parent but is instead given to

the parentified child, these children do not have the maturity to be authority figures for their siblings.

2. Parentified children are overloaded with tasks or are not given age-appropriate responsibilities. This fosters feelings of helplessness and failure, prevents recuperation from being overworked, and denies opportunities for interactions with peers.

3. Rules and roles are not made clear to the children; they do not have clear expectations about their behavior, their responsibilities, and the consequences of misbehaving.

4. Parents do not spend quality time with their children. When they are not given nurturing and support, children feel abandoned, neglected, and lonely.

In short, using parentified children in caretaking roles works well only when authority remains with the parents, the children are given reasonable and age-appropriate responsibilities, rules and roles are clear to everyone, and the children receive attention and care from their parents.

Pathological Shaming

Shame is the unpleasant emotion we experience when we believe that we have behaved or acted inappropriately. It is normal and healthy when it is associated with meeting reasonable expectations and focused on our actions. Shame motivates us to take corrective steps toward behaving in a manner that is culturally and socially acceptable. Equally important, it guards us against narcissism, fosters sensitivity toward those around us, and promotes ethical and moral conduct. However, shame can be pathological when it promotes negative feelings because we are unable to meet unrealistic expectations or when it focuses on our physical, personal, and emotional attributes, on who we are rather than what we do.

Common examples of pathological shame in Chinese families include making a child feel bad for being unable to enter college even when he or she does not have the cognitive ability to do so, for being born a girl instead of a boy, or for having a mental illness. Such shame is extremely damaging because, with the exception of hiding or not existing, individuals cannot take any corrective actions to rectify matters.

Triangulation

Triangulation is the process of drawing a third person into a two-person system to help reduce anxiety or conflict. In Chinese families, for example, it is common for parents to be drawn into settling marital disputes. In treatment recently, a wife called her mother-in-law to ask her to stop her husband's infidelity and get him to come home after work instead of going gambling. Her husband became infuriated when he learned from his parents of his wife's actions. In highly conflictual families, numerous overlapping triangles involve both family and nonfamily members.

Such relationships are very dysfunctional because they inevitably exacerbate rather than reduce conflict, foster resentment, and create disloyalty. They also disregard appropriate boundary keeping and role expectations, undermine hierarchy and authority, and perpetuate unfairness and disrespect.

Favoritism

Favoritism, no matter who is favored, can be damaging to a family by promoting resentment, sibling rivalry, and unfairness. Those who are treated unfavorably often develop deep insecurities, feeling unloved, worthless, and discounted. In many Chinese families, favoritism or preferential treatment is given to sons, who are viewed in Chinese culture as having a higher value than daughters because, among other things, they carry on the family name.

Children who experience jealousy over favoritism they have observed may act out their angry feelings by behaving oppositionally; others seek status by joining gangs or demand special attention by acting obnoxiously. Still others try to get love and attention from their parents by becoming emotionally ill.

Sixteen-year-old Karen was brought to see me because of depression, social isolation, and a suicide attempt. The basis for her problems was her belief that her brother, Mark, was favored and received all the attention at home, especially with her mother. She was given many responsibilities at home while he had none. He was allowed to be out with friends while she had to remain at home; he was given a car at the age of sixteen while she was not. She believed that when they visited Taiwan, he was doted on by his paternal grandmother and she and her sister Linnea were treated with indifference. Fortunately, I was able to help Karen by helping her parents learn to treat all their children fairly.

Intergenerational Cultural Conflict

Probably the most common problem among Chinese families is intergenerational cultural conflict, in which children rebel against the Chinese norms and values their parents try to impose on them. In identifying with Western society, children find their parents' child-rearing practices either outdated, restrictive, insensitive to their needs, or punitive. In treatment, parent-child conflicts are often the result of children wanting more autonomy and independence and parents wanting the opposite. The Lee family case described in Chapters Five and Six will illustrate the kinds of problems such families are confronted with and how they are addressed in treatment.

Unwillingness to Compromise

Children will generally respond to their parents the same way they are treated. If they are spoken to with kindness, understanding, and fairness, they will respond in kind. However, this is normally not the case when families enter therapy. Feeling angry, frustrated, and helpless, parents may be closed-minded and unwilling to change, negotiate differences, or be open to the thoughts, ideas, and convictions of their children.

This unwillingness to compromise is further exacerbated in Chinese families because of their hierarchical and authoritarian nature. Issues between parents and children are not mediated; instead, children are expected to obey the instructions given to them. Consequently, it is often difficult to help Chinese parents to be open and sensitive to the thoughts, feelings, and concerns of their children.

Guiding Principles of Practice

To effectively address the issues brought to treatment by Chinese families, therapists using CAFT must have an enormous body of knowledge and numerous clinical skills. We must be able to establish a cooperative therapeutic relationship, assess and reassess the needs of our clients, establish a comprehensive and effective treatment plan, monitor our clients' progress in treatment, alter treatment plans if necessary, and evaluate therapeutic outcomes. While focusing on these tasks, we must establish and maintain trust, work through resistance, and be sensitive and supportive of our clients' vulnerabilities.

The therapeutic process can be very intense and highly charged, with clients who are suicidal, extremely angry, or very argumentative. Although there may be some similarities, each client or family is different, with different problems and family configurations, interactional patterns, personalities, and levels of motivation. Each case can present new challenges and opportunities for learning and for both professional and personal growth. However, the complexity of treatment, with its numerous tasks and variables that have to be taken into consideration, can confuse and overwhelm therapists, especially those who are inexperienced. In addition to following the guidelines in the models presented at the beginning of this chapter, therapists using CAFT can prevent this from happening by using this set of practice principles:

1. Create and maintain a positive treatment atmosphere.
2. Join with clients.
3. Support the family's hierarchical structure.
4. Accept the role of authority figure.
5. Accept the role of expert.
6. Accept the role of change agent.
7. Accept the role of educator.
8. Maintain neutrality.
9. Foster the participation of all family members.
10. Work from critical to less critical issues.
11. Keep therapy moving.
12. Be flexible and creative.

These principles of practice provide a framework for conducting interviews in a planned, structured, and orderly fashion. They reflect the assumptions on which CAFT is based, the role of therapists, and the way therapy should be conducted. They are applied in each session and stage throughout the clinical process.

Create and Maintain a Positive Treatment Atmosphere

Many clients enter treatment feeling apprehensive, fearful, and vulnerable, not knowing what to expect or how they will be judged. Others, particularly mandated clients who have been accused of wrongdoing, feel guilty, ashamed, or defective. Consequently, it is important for therapists using CAFT to provide a positive and safe atmosphere in which our clients can feel comfortable and open to change. A negative therapeutic environment will only stifle growth by fostering resentment, defensiveness, and resistance.

Creating a positive treatment milieu is a continual process and can be accomplished in any number of ways. These include

- Speaking in a warm and accepting manner
- Giving everyone an equal opportunity to speak
- Reframing negative perceptions into positive ones
- Highlighting strengths rather than weaknesses
- Reinforcing positive behavior
- Identifying with the clients' concerns
- Addressing everyone's issues
- Creating positive interactions
- Using language and concepts that are familiar and have meaning to clients

Together, these interventions convey to our clients that they are important, understood, respected, and accepted for being themselves.

Join with Clients

It is important for therapists using CAFT to join with our clients, which involves more than just establishing a therapeutic relationship. We must make an active effort to demonstrate to clients that we care for them, understand and empathize with their pain and confusion, and are like them in many ways. Joining can take place overtly or covertly. Overt joining, for example, can be accomplished by disclosing something about ourselves or verbally expressing sympathy for an issue the client is addressing. Covert joining can be conveyed by talking to clients in the manner to which they are accustomed—formally, politely, and with emotional reserve.

Support the Family's Hierarchical Structure

Therapists using CAFT should respect and work within the hierarchical structure of the Chinese family. We support the parents' authority and right to make decisions for their children and to establish rules and expectations for their lives. However, we also believe that children have a right to be understood and heard. Consequently, we encourage children to share their thoughts and feelings with their parents and help the parents to be receptive to what is shared.

Accept the Role of Authority Figure

Authority derives from power, but the two are not synonymous. Power is the capacity to directly or indirectly control the behavior of others through manipulation, whereas authority, the established right to make decisions on pertinent issues, is a transactional concept that includes the consent of another person who is responsive to that authority.

Chinese clients view the therapeutic relationship as being hierarchical, with the position of authority given to us. We accept this position and, with their implicit consent, we control sessions, establish boundaries, and assert ourselves in organizing the information presented in a manner that is useful in establishing clearly defined treatment goals and plans to achieve them. In some circumstances we use our authority to exercise power. In cases of child abuse, for example, we tell clients that they are not permitted to harm their children physically.

The inappropriate use of authority can be detrimental. We are careful to guard against being authoritarian and dictatorial because we recognize that everyone wishes to be treated with honor and respect. Experience has shown us that if we lose sight of this fact, clients may not challenge us in the session; they simply will not return.

Accept the Role of Expert

With Chinese clients, when we accept the role of expert we foster credibility and instill a sense of confidence in what we do. Our expertness can be conveyed implicitly by providing useful information, helping clients to clarify and pinpoint issues, and projecting an image of self-confidence. It can also be conveyed explicitly by sharing, in an unobtrusive and sensitive manner, our agency's position, our educational credentials, or our professional experiences.

I convey to my clients within the first ten minutes of an interview that I am a professor and that I have been providing treatment for over twenty years. Establishing credibility does not automatically lead to successful outcomes, but it does provide a good foundation upon which to begin treatment by fostering trust, cooperation, and participation on the part of our clients.

Accept the Role of Change Agent

In the role of change agent, we work actively rather than passively in the treatment process. The emphasis is not just on understanding but on action, which is what Chinese families expect from treatment. In fact, we attempt to facilitate a change in the first session, no matter how small it may be. This change can be a feeling, attitude, perception, or behavior. Any positive changes can work toward empowering clients and fostering feelings of competency, movement, and hopefulness. They also instill trust and credibility in us and the treatment process.

Accept the Role of Educator

Chinese clients see our role as similar to that of a physician and expect to be educated about what is causing their problems and what can and should be done to alleviate them. We therefore provide information, share our perceptions, give answers, and make suggestions. However, we must avoid lecturing to our clients or admonishing them for inappropriate behaviors. We must also be careful to provide information in a manner that doesn't make them feel ashamed, stupid, inferior, or inadequate.

Maintain Neutrality

It is important to maintain neutrality in sessions. Siding with one member of the family triangulates us into the conflict, alienating those we are siding against and making them angry. More importantly, we lose trust and credibility with everyone, including the person with whom we have sided. This renders us ineffective, because everyone will believe that our thoughts and opinions are purely subjective and based on who tells the more convincing story, rather than on clinical experience and professional judgment. Furthermore, losing our neutrality can be seen to reflect a lack of skills, insensitivity, immaturity, a lack of sound judgment, or countertransference.

Foster the Participation of All Family Members

Family therapy with Chinese families is generally more successful when everyone is involved in the treatment process. This is accomplished first by inviting to each session only those with whom we are going to work. Once the session begins, we can use any number of interventions to foster participation and interaction. These include preventing any one family member from dominating the discussion, blocking intrusions when someone is speaking, and encouraging quiet members to contribute. In some instances, a cotherapist can assist us in working with different subgroups simultaneously or can give tasks to some clients while we work with others.

Work from Critical to Less Critical Issues

Chinese families often come to treatment with multiple problems. For example, they may simultaneously be dealing with a crisis; a major family dispute; the need for financial assistance, employment, medical care, or psychiatric care for a severely depressed family member; and a child who is in danger of being expelled from school. In the problem stage of the initial interview, the issues should be examined systematically, ranked in the order of importance, and worked on one problem at a time. We should work generally from more critical to less critical issues and from difficult to easy ones.

The issues should be addressed in the following order:

1. The crisis (for example, the death of a loved one, rape, or any form of violence)

2. Situational or adjustment issues (for example, finding and acquiring needed medical care, employment, housing, or educational programs)

3. Interpersonal problems (for example, intergenerational differences, oppositional behavior, or school-related problems)

4. Chronic or long-standing problems (for example, addiction, mental illness, or severe marital conflicts)

When we follow these guidelines, clients feel that issues are manageable. As problems become resolved, they learn to apply the knowledge and skills they have gained to successfully negotiate their other difficulties.

Keep Therapy Moving

CAFT requires the therapist to keep the therapeutic process moving and avoid unproductive interventions and use of time. We must therefore be careful to stay focused on treatment goals and not let ourselves be sidetracked by personal issues or issues that don't have a direct bearing on the needs of the family. We must work on negotiable rather than nonnegotiable issues, focus on resolving problems rather than looking for truths, and go with resistance rather than trying to fight through it. We must also help parents avoid struggles with their children that they cannot bring to a successful resolution, because such encounters serve no purpose other than to make those involved feel more helpless, frustrated, and angry.

Be Flexible and Creative

Although sessions are highly structured and well planned, therapists using CAFT need to recognize that the therapeutic process is dynamic and unpredictable, requiring flexibility and creativity. We must be able to adapt to the idiosyncratic responses to treatment and unique needs of each of our clients, rather than forcing them to fit our rigid principles and procedures.

Therapy is a process of trial and error, with each unsuccessful intervention being turned into a diagnostic tool for devising the next intercession. We know that an intervention may be successful with one client but ineffective with another. We must therefore have a wide range of interventions from which to choose if we are going to be effective in helping our clients.

Therapy requires a broad knowledge base, intervention skills, and the use of many principles of practice to guide the treatment process. It is a collaborative process and little can be accomplished without the cooperation and support of our clients. As therapists, we do not have control over our clients. Instead, they allow us to influence them. Karen didn't have to speak and her parents didn't have to cooperate. Change occurred because the family welcomed my assistance. I believe that they welcomed it because they felt safe in treatment, experienced my admiration and concern for them, respected my clinical skills, and were genuinely concerned about one another's well-being. The next chapter will describe six practice models that are compatible with and can augment CAFT in helping Chinese American families.

Chapter Four

Adjusting the Western Lens

Selecting Appropriate Treatment Models

This chapter describes six major clinical models that are compatible with CAFT and can be used in conjunction with it. They are (1) Structural Family Therapy, (2) Strategic Therapy, (3) Planned Short-Term Treatment, (4) Rational-Emotive Therapy, (5) Solution Focused Therapy, and (6) Contextual Family Therapy. These models, along with general systems theory, case management, crisis intervention, and social learning theory, described in Chapter Three, provide therapists with a multidimensional and comprehensive framework for diagnosing and treating Chinese families.

Using the six models presented in this chapter allows therapists to be more creative and to have a broader range of interventions from which to choose. It also allows us to adapt to the expectations of clients and the style in which they work best. Although the major objective of treatment is to assist clients in achieving family integration by resolving the issues they bring to treatment, it may be better to focus on solutions with some families, to work with others strategically, and to work with still others cognitively. Thus, we can use the model that best suits our clients' needs.

Structural Family Therapy

Structural Family Therapy was developed by Salvador Minuchin and his colleagues at the Philadelphia Child Guidance Clinic to serve ethnic minority and low-income families in the neighborhoods of Philadelphia (Minuchin and others, 1967; Minuchin, 1974). Since its inception, the model has been applied to numerous areas of practice including work with psychosomatic illness, children of divorce, single-parent households, and Chinese families. The model incorporates both general systems theory and ecological theory, but its central concept is *family structure*, which Aponte and VanDeusen (1981) define as follows:

> [Family] structure refers to the regulating codes as manifested in the operational patterns through which people relate to one another in order to carry out functions. These functions are the modes of action by which the system fulfills its purpose and the operations are those functions actualized in specific activities. The members of the system structure their relationships in accordance with the requirements of each operation [p. 312].

Structural family therapists diagnose families according to the boundary keeping of subgroups within the family. Subgroups can be based upon any number of factors including generation, role, function, sex, or interest. Common subgroups are husband-wife or marital, grandparent, sibling, and parent-child. There is also what is called an executive subgroup, consisting of a single parent and a child elevated to the position of a parentified child. The subgroups are defined by boundaries or rules that prescribe who should be in contact with whom about what. Examples of boundaries in Chinese families are the rules prescribing that children need to respect and honor their parents and that parents should model ethical behavior for their children. Boundaries are put on a continuum, with rigid boundaries at one end that lead to disengagement, clear boundaries in the middle, and diffuse boundaries on the other end that lead to enmeshment. Different subgroups have different boundaries. Dysfunctional families normally show a severe breakdown of one or more of the subgroups within the family (Minuchin, 1974).

Structural Family Therapy, like CAFT, recognizes, respects, and reinforces the hierarchical nature of families. In addition, it is a problem-centered approach, addressing issues concretely and pragmatically. Therapists are concerned about what is happening in the present rather than what happened in the past. The emphasis in treatment is on fostering permeability in rigid boundaries and strengthening diffuse ones. In addition to addressing boundary issues, therapy is task-centered, focused on helping clients to acquire the skills, resources, or services needed to improve their living conditions. As a result, treatment tends to be short-term, lasting from six to ten sessions (Aponte and VanDeusen, 1981, p. 324).

The role of structural family therapists is to act as facilitators for change. They actively participate in treatment, helping to empower rather than create dependency, support rather than criticize, guide rather than tell, and find solutions rather than talk about what created the problems. Therapists are free to use a wide range of methods for intervening, including cognitive, affective, behavioral, and strategic methods. Furthermore, treatment is not necessarily based on the fifty-minute hour, but on doing whatever it takes to assist family members in meeting their needs. Consequently, structural family therapists take on many roles.

Implications for Treatment

Structural Family Therapy is ideally suited for working with Chinese families and is compatible with CAFT. Its conceptual framework is closely aligned with CAFT's and with the way the traditional Chinese family is constituted. It is a family therapy approach that recognizes and respects the importance of hierarchy, maintenance of generational boundaries, recognition of parents as authority figures, and the need for clearly defined roles. Like CAFT, it is a process-oriented approach that works toward interpersonal compromise based on having members talk to one another in a positive reciprocal manner. Furthermore, it is an approach that facilitates change rather than simply talking about it. Finally, it conforms with the Chinese expectation that counseling should be active, task- and problem-centered, and brief.

Structural Family Therapy and CAFT incorporate ecological theory, which encourages therapists to go beyond providing clinical interventions. Structural family therapists, like therapists using CAFT, also provide advocacy, education, and mediation, services often needed by Chinese families. In addition, therapists are free to assist clients in obtaining necessary programs and resources.

The model's flexibility allows therapists to be creative and unconventional in their interventions, something that is very useful in working with Chinese families. For example, I have held clinical sessions at a client's apartment during breakfast because the father had been temporarily laid off and could not continue to pay for my services. I did this so that he could save face and repay the debt he believed he owed me.

The therapist's role as an authority figure engenders honor and respect from Chinese clients, encouraging them to continue in treatment. At the same time, the emphasis on developing strengths and becoming empowered also allows clients to feel respected and honored. In addition, they feel safe, retain their dignity, and use their own inner resources and innate abilities to resolve problems and concerns.

The incorporation of general systems theory allows structural family therapists, like therapists using CAFT, to work with any subgroup within the family, recognizing, as indicated previously, that a change in one part of the system often leads to changes in other parts. They also recognize that major changes do not necessarily have to happen for first-order or primary changes to take place. Small changes can automatically lead to larger ones, so families that are already bearing a great deal of stress and are overextended do not experience the added burden put on them by some other models.

Strategic Therapy

The form of Strategic Therapy presented in this section is the approach developed by Jay Haley, a pioneer in the family therapy movement, and presented in his classic book, *Problem-Solving Therapy* (1987). Haley worked with many prominent individuals in the field of therapy, including Gregory Bateson, John Weakland, Don

D. Jackson, Milton Erickson, and Salvador Minuchin. Because of his long collaboration with Minuchin at the Philadelphia Child Guidance Clinic, Structural Therapy and Strategic Therapy have much in common and are often combined.

Strategic Therapy is based on communication theory, and although it is concerned with family dynamics, it is more concerned with the negative interactional sequence of behaviors between particular individuals, whether or not they are related, or between an individual and his or her particular circumstances (for example, the inability of an individual to pass a test). Thus, Strategic Therapy is applicable to working not only with families but with individuals, couples, and groups as well. Presenting problems are viewed as being based in faulty or dysfunctional communication patterns.

According to communication theory, there are two types of communication—digital and analogic. Digital communication takes place through words that are assigned specific meanings; in analogic communication, which constitutes most of what is expressed, the idea or thing being communicated is transmitted nonverbally in a representational manner. This includes how and when things are said, facial expressions, bodily gestures, tone of voice, and so on. Communication theory has three axioms: (1) all behavior is communication, and therefore it is impossible not to communicate; (2) a communication not only conveys information but also generally contains a command; and (3) communication is a cybernetic or transactional process and, in the interchange, each response contains the preceding communication (Haley, 1987).

Faulty communication patterns can be manifested in countless ways. For example, inappropriate communication can take place when the analogic message does not match the content of the digital statement (a person smiles when he is expressing anger). In negating messages, case messages that are sent are nullified ("What you're telling me can't be true"). In disconfirming responses, the receiver of the message is not concerned with the truth or falsehood of the sender's statement but instead negates the sender as a source of information ("You are stupid for thinking that").

It is the task of strategic therapists to identify negative circular communication patterns and use interventions, many of which are strategically introduced to disrupt these patterns. The negative patterns are referred to as symptoms, or particular types of behavior functioning as homeostatic mechanisms that regulate family interactions. Strategic therapists assume that a disruption in the negative communication pattern will unsettle the family's homeostatic balance. It is hoped that this will force members involved in the interaction to find new and positive ways to communicate, behave, and restore homeostasis. This often results in the removal of the original symptoms.

Let's take the Chin family as an example. Mr. and Mrs. Chin were referred to me because their fourteen-year-old daughter, Joan, was beginning to suffer from anorexia nervosa. Mr. Chin was seldom home, working as a waiter until 2:00 A.M. and spending time with friends before going to work. Mrs. Chin had the primary responsibility for raising Joan and her sixteen-year-old brother, Tim. Both parents were ineffective in getting Joan to eat. I immediately supported Joan's fear of becoming obese, the reason she gave for refusing to eat. I next disengaged both parents from the negative circular pattern surrounding the power struggle over eating, telling them that because I was an expert on anorexia, I would take the responsibility for Joan's diet. I told Joan that I would bring in a dietitian to help regulate her weight but wouldn't do so until she began acting responsibly. I then proceeded to assist Mrs. Chin in resolving other problems she had with her daughter. A few days later, seeking a new way to engage her parents, Joan began sneaking food out of the refrigerator. Shortly afterward, with the assistance of the dietitian, Joan began to eat regularly. During the course of treatment, it was learned that her unwillingness to eat was symptomatic of a deeper issue, consisting of several disputes related to intergenerational cultural differences between Joan and her parents. Through the use of cognitive-restructuring, solution-focused, and behavioral interventions, those differences were negotiated successfully. Treatment ended after nine sessions.

This case illustrates many of the principles involved in Strategic Therapy. First, I acted as an expert and change agent and was in control of treatment. Second, treatment was symptom-oriented, and therefore the focus remained on the presenting problems. There was no assumption that I knew the "real problem." Third, the negative circular mother-daughter pattern surrounding eating was quickly observed and disrupted, forcing Joan to seek a different way to engage her parents. Fourth, support for the parents' hierarchical position was maintained while the needs of the child were heard. Fifth, I worked to empower both the mother and the daughter. The father was unavailable for therapy; however, Strategic Therapy does not require all family members to be present because of the general systems theory principle that states that change in one part of the system generally leads to changes in other parts. Finally, the therapy was active and directive: through homework assignments and enactments in the session, Mrs. Chin and Joan learned to communicate effectively and resolve their differences.

Implications for Treatment

Strategic Therapy requires the therapist to be astute at tracking communication patterns on several levels, assertive, and willing to be manipulative, directive, and challenging in a positive manner. For those who can master its principles, it is a very powerful means of helping individuals, couples, and families.

Strategic Therapy is compatible with CAFT and with working with Chinese families because, like Structural Family Therapy, it respects hierarchy, the maintenance of intergenerational boundaries, and clarity of roles. Chinese also like the fact that the therapists are authority figures, directive, and in charge of treatment. And its concrete, pragmatic, and problem-centered approach to resolving issues is congruent with the way that Chinese solve problems and therapists using CAFT work. Finally, because it tries to empower clients and share positive interpretations of behaviors and attitudes, the clients appreciate the respect and honor they are shown during their treatment.

What is especially useful to Chinese families is the ability of strategic therapists to work at the *metalevel* or indirectly. Working in this manner allows therapists to address touchy or important issues without fostering shame or embarrassment, something to which Chinese are highly sensitive. For example, we might educate parents indirectly by saying to their children, "Your parents know that harsh corporal punishment leads to feelings of fear, intimidation, and the desire to rebel or be disobedient." Or, to improve an obviously conflictual marriage, we might help couples to work together as parents to resolve their children's oppositional behaviors. When parents work together cooperatively to address the problems of their children, in addition to gaining insights and learning skills, they may also improve their marital relationship.

Planned Short-Term Treatment

Richard A. Wells's *Planned Short-Term Treatment* (1982) represents one of several brief approaches to individual, couple, and family therapy. The rationale for such approaches is the assumption that clients wish to resolve their problems as quickly as possible and spend the least amount of time in treatment, which is viewed as an infringement on their daily life. This is evidenced in part by the fact that regardless of whether the setting is a family service agency, child guidance clinic, or mental health center, nearly 80 percent of the clients will spend fewer than six sessions in treatment (Beck and Jones, 1973; Parad, 1968; Verny, 1970).

Brief therapies tend to be active, goal-oriented, and task-centered. They work in a concrete rather than an abstract manner, remain focused on the present rather than on the past, and center primarily on change rather than on understanding. Interviews are very structured, purposeful, and focused on creating immediate changes. Most are time-limited, with contracts lasting for six to twelve sessions.

Planned Short-Term Treatment attempts to be broad in its conceptual framework, incorporating crisis intervention theory, social learning theory, interpersonal relationship or family theory, and ego psychology. Thus, it attempts to address individuals in relation to their ability to cope effectively with stress or crisis, learn appropriate ways of relating and behaving, establish nurturing and supportive family relationships, and find ways to establish a positive ego. It is a time-limited model, with one or two sessions used for assessment and establishment of goals, up to fifteen sessions for achieving stated goals, and a follow-up session two to four months after termination. The model is eclectic in its approach but relies heavily on cognitive-behavioral interventions.

In the initial interviews, the goal of therapists is to foster hope, demonstrate genuine concern for the feelings and problems of their clients, identify one or two problems that need to be addressed, define treatment goals, and establish a therapeutic contract with a time frame in which to work. Wells borrows from Reid and Epstein (1972) in outlining the following seven categories of concern or "problems of living" that may need to be addressed: (1) interpersonal conflict, (2) dissatisfaction with social relationships, (3) difficulties in role performance; (4) reactive emotional distress (for Chinese this may include physical distress), (5) problems of social transition, (6) problems with formal organizations, and (7) inadequate resources.

Once problems of living have been identified in the initial session, issues are organized into specific goals with measurable outcomes. Practice principles at this time include keeping tasks simple, working in sequences and segments, and focusing on making incremental changes. For example, the first step in helping a mother whose angry daughter is not complying with her wishes may be to work briefly with the daughter to defuse her anger. If this is successful, it will allow her to be receptive to her mother's communication. Next, the therapist acts as an interpreter, passing on messages between the mother and daughter. In this manner, the therapist can continue to defuse conflicts and reframe negative perceptions into positive ones, creating an atmosphere of care and concern rather than one of indifference and animosity. The therapist can then encourage the clients to talk with one another, carefully monitoring the situation and encouraging a positive reciprocal interaction. The emphasis at this stage is on understanding, not on changing. After the issues have been made clear, the mother and daughter are encouraged to negotiate differences and find a compromise.

Planned Short-Term Treatment is a literal approach to working with clients. The focus is therefore on educational skill building and effective communication. If clients feel stressful, they are taught relaxation techniques. If they need various services, they are taught how to find them and how to overcome any possible obstructions they might encounter. If they are fearful about an upcoming job interview, they are shown how to effectively participate in one through role playing. Therapy is active, using enactments during sessions and homework between sessions.

Implications for Treatment

Chinese families hope or expect that treatment will be brief, practical, and goal-, problem-, and task-centered. Planned Short-Term Treatment is another model that can be used in conjunction with CAFT to help meet their needs. Organizing issues around "problems of living" rather than intrapersonal or interpersonal deficits helps to reduce the shame that many Chinese experience when seeking treatment. The emphasis on providing hope is extremely helpful in countering or reversing the feelings of helplessness and despair that clients often experience at the beginning of treatment. And the emphasis on skill building is particularly useful to immigrants, who lack so many of the skills required to be successful in this country. Finally, demonstrating genuine concern for their well-being allows clients to feel normal, respected, and supported.

Rational-Emotive Therapy

Rational-Emotive Therapy is one of several cognitive therapeutic approaches to working with individuals, couples, and families.

These approaches begin with the theoretical premise that emotions and behaviors are based on how individuals, over a period of time and through their experiences, cognitively structure or construct their world. Cognitive therapists attribute problems to faulty thinking. Consequently, the emphasis in treatment is on cognitive restructuring, or helping clients to change distorted, unrealistic, and dysfunctional thoughts into correct, reasonable, and appropriate ones.

Cognitive therapists believe that the following five types of interrelated cognitive attributes influence the development and maintenance of individuals' beliefs about what happens in the world: (1) assumptions, (2) standards, (3) perceptions, (4) attributes, and (5) expectancies (Baucom and Epstein, 1990). Assumptions are suppositions about the way people and relationships are, and standards are beliefs about the way they should be.

Chinese parents assume loyalty from their children, which is believed by many to be reflected in absolute obedience. Perceptions relate to the way individuals comprehend their physical and social environment, attributes to their beliefs about why things happen, and expectancies to their predictions about what will occur in the future. Faulty or dysfunctional thinking can develop among any of these characteristics. Individuals can have wrong assumptions, make unreasonable demands, misperceive the truth, draw wrong conclusions, and make wrong projections.

Although Rational-Emotive Therapy recognizes the importance of these five attributes, it focuses primarily on the identification and modification of irrational standards and on the consequences when those standards are not met (Wessler and Wessler, 1980). This practice is based on the belief that no matter how things are perceived or interpreted, it is what happens when expectations are not met that creates dysfunctional emotional and behavioral responses. The model also recognizes the importance of family dynamics but chooses to focus on changing the perceptions of individual members, rather than on modifying inappropriate transactional patterns. Finally, Rational-Emotive Therapy believes that it is not a lack of communication skills that creates problems, but the irrational cognitions that block effective use of them. In fact, an individual may communicate very effectively, but if the receiver of the message distorts or is not receptive to what the sender is conveying, angry feelings and behaviors can still erupt. An adolescent son, for example, may state very clearly why he wishes to become an automobile mechanic rather than go on to college, but his father may remain angry and believe that his son is being defiant if his mind is fixed on his son's attending college.

Rational-Emotive Therapy is symptom-oriented, concrete, short-term, directive, and practical. It is a clearly defined model that approaches treatment through the use of an "ABC" method. "A" represents activating events, "B" represents beliefs regarding those events, and "C" stands for the emotional and behavioral consequences of those beliefs. In addition, "D" represents the process of disputing or challenging dysfunctional perceptions and "E" is a more rational, effective new philosophy to help clients address difficult issues more reasonably (Ellis and others, 1989). Rational-Emotive Therapy is an active approach, with clients being asked, among other things, to complete homework assignments, participate in role playing, or attend parent education or assertive training classes. Specific goals for therapy are established and sessions are planned with specific outcomes in mind. Finally, although they are not necessary, behavioral interventions are generally integrated into the treatment plan.

Unfortunately, many therapists are inadequately trained in the use of cognitive interventions and therefore are prone to make the following mistakes (Beck, Rush, Shaw, and Emery, 1979):

1. They may be overly reductionistic and simplistic, giving clients shallow and commonsense responses to complex and difficult issues.

2. They may be overly didactic or excessively interpretive, forgetting that clients will remember very little of what was presented in the session.

3. They may be too superficial, forgetting to explore issues sufficiently before developing and initiating appropriate interventions.

4. They may be misled into readily accepting intellectual insights before the client has emotionally internalized what was presented.

5. They may be naive, believing that insights will automatically lead to changes.

6. They may slip into becoming patronizing, treating clients as if they were stupid, ignorant, or inferior.

Well-trained rational-emotive therapists, however, do not make these mistakes and instead work with clients collaboratively to monitor, question, examine, and challenge unreasonable, illogical, and self-defeating attitudes. They also teach clients to substitute more reality-oriented standards for their biased cognitions. In so doing, they recognize the importance of emotions in individuals and in the therapeutic process. In fact, the significance of emotions is reflected in part by the model's name change from Rational Therapy to Rational-Emotive Therapy. Therapists are sensitive to their clients' feelings and attempt to provide a warm, safe, and sensitive therapeutic environment in which change can occur. Although the major emphasis is on cognitive restructuring, clients are encouraged to identify, express, and understand their feelings and their interconnectedness with perceptions and behaviors.

Implications for Treatment

Rational-Emotive Therapy is another model that is ideally compatible with CAFT because it is cognitively rather than emotionally oriented; it expects treatment to be brief, active, and informative; and it perceives therapists as being educators. The model's ABC approach is practical and matches the manner in which Chinese solve problems and seek answers to their questions. It works directly and effectively with one of the major issues faced by Chinese immigrants—negotiating differences between the assumptions, standards, perceptions, attributes, and expectancies of their culture of origin and those of the culture of their adopted country. Rational-Emotive Therapy provides a safe therapeutic climate in which these differences can be examined in a logical and empirical manner.

I believe that Rational-Emotive Therapy interventions are especially useful in helping to change four cognitive distortions that are commonly observed in Chinese families: (1) personalization, (2) dichotomous thinking, (3) overgeneralization, and (4) magnification. These, like all distortions, are failures in the process of gathering and utilizing data regardless of the particular content of that information. Thus, they bias individuals' perceptions of events, interactional patterns, and motives.

Personalization is the act of taking credit or responsibility for things beyond one's control. For example, poor immigrant parents often feel ashamed of their inability, through no fault of their own, to provide adequately for their children. *Dichotomous thinking* is the state of perceiving things in absolutes: right and wrong or black and white. In dichotomous thinking, a father may believe that his wife is spoiling their children because she is flexible with them. In *overgeneralization*, individuals draw sweeping or broad conclusions based on a few experiences or little information. A mother, for example, may conclude that her daughter will never succeed in college and is irresponsible because she had a B grade-point average instead of an A and refuses to adequately clean her room. *Magnification* consists of overestimating or exaggerating the significance of an event or experience. A father may believe that his son is completely disrespectful because he became angry with a teacher he believed was treating him unfairly and refused to do an assignment for him.

Rational-Emotive Therapy can help to rectify both these four distortions and any other dysfunctional or irrational thought patterns. It has been applied to many problem areas brought to treatment by Chinese American families, including depression, parent-child conflicts, and drug and alcohol abuse. Although it relies heavily on cognitive techniques such as definition of beliefs, label shifting, philosophical shifts, logical fallacies, and alternative interpretations, the model has the flexibility to incorporate behavioral, strategic, or other therapeutic interventions in the treatment plan.

Solution Focused Therapy

Solution Focused Therapy represents an optimistic and proactive approach to treatment. It tracks positive attributes or interactions, examines strengths, and works to empower clients. Rather than focusing on problems and deficits, it encourages individuals to envision their goals and focus on their talents and skills. Clients are taught to use resources they already possess in order to change problematic situations. As a result, they experience concrete successes quickly.

Solution Focused Therapy is rooted in the brief and strategic approaches to individual and family therapy developed at the Mental Research Institute in Palo Alto, California, and in the work of Milton Erickson and Gregory Bateson. Major contributors to the model include Steve de Shazer, Insoo Berg Kim, William Hanlon, Michele Weiner-Davis, John L. Walter, and Jane E. Peller. Its goals are to solve immediate complaints by helping clients to do something different or think differently, therefore becoming more content with their life. The theoretical underpinning for the model is constructivist theory, which postulates that individuals construct and reconstruct their realities as they proceed through life. Solution-focused therapists, therefore, conclude that their clients, not the therapists, are the experts on their problems. In fact, they believe that one of the problems in treatment is that therapists using theoretical formulations impose their reality onto their clients.

Solution Focused Therapy addresses strengths rather than weaknesses and solutions rather than problems, looking to the future rather than to the past. The major premise on which the model rests is that although clients may have lost sight of their abilities, they have the resources and skills to solve their problems. The task of the therapist, therefore, is to assist them in rediscovering their lost or hidden talents. In addition, Solution Focused Therapy assumes that small changes lead to bigger ones, believes that therapists should intervene as little as possible, and uses language to foster change. In fact, the therapy is based on "solution talk," or the raising of questions that guide clients to solutions. The aim of treatment is to deconstruct the problem by allowing clients to discuss only what works and is useful. Therapists do not judge their clients' solutions, as long as they seem to be satisfactory to the individual, couple, or family.

The model follows a formula approach that uses tasks or assignments that are believed to be universally effective regardless of the problem. Treatment is focused on having therapists ask the following series of questions directed toward the issues the clients have brought to treatment:

1. Presuppositional questions
2. The miracle question
3. Exception questions
4. Scaling questions
5. Coping and presession change questions

Toward the end of each session, therapists take a brief break and plan a message to deliver to their clients that includes acknowledgment and validation of their situation and their strengths, a bridging statement, and a task that will encourage them to find solutions to the presenting issues.

Presuppositional questions help to reorient clients away from a negative focus and toward a positive one. They ignore the client's view of the problem by phrasing questions in a manner that offers solutions. A parent whose adolescent son is performing poorly in school, for example, may be asked, "When your son begins to do well in school, what will he and the rest of the family be doing at home that is different?" Family members will be asked to elaborate on the question. The solutions are implicit in the answers.

The *miracle question* is "Suppose that one night, while you were asleep, there was a miracle and this problem was solved. How would you know and what would be different?" This question activates a problem-solving mindset by giving people a clear vision of their goals and what is required to achieve them. Therapists can encourage them to do those things despite the problem, rendering it less significant. The crystal-ball technique, which requires the client to look into the future and describe what life would be like without the problem, has a similar purpose.

Exception questions explore the times when the problem did not exist. By studying what was different about those times, clients discover what they can do to expand such exceptions. Therapists can then highlight those differences and encourage the clients to behave in accordance with them. A parent whose child is acting oppositional, for example, may be asked, "When your son is behaving respectfully, what is happening between the two of you?" Again, implicit in the answer is the solution or what needs to occur if change is to take place.

Scaling questions are used because they are thought to be very simple, useful, and versatile. They are quantitative, in that clients are asked to place their responses on a scale of 1 to 10. These questions are used as a baseline to measure change. A father whose child is behaving irresponsibly, for example, may be asked, "On a scale of 1 to 10, 1 meaning somewhat responsible and 10 very responsible, how responsible was your son today?" Following the answer, the therapist asks, "What would it take for him to demonstrate that he has moved up the scale by half a point?" By listening to his father's answer, the child hears part of the solution to making his father satisfied with his behavior. If change does occur, it can be measured on the imaginary scale and the family members can experience movement.

Coping and presession change questions challenge the belief that a situation is hopeless. By highlighting what clients have done on their own, they imply that small changes may already have happened. A mother whose daughter is argumentative about doing household chores may be asked how she coped with her daughter's disrespectful behavior during the week. Her answer may show that she has done something constructive and therefore has some power over the situation.

Implications for Treatment

Solution Focused Therapy in its pure form does not lend itself to working with traditional Chinese families. The refusal of solution-focused therapists to be authority figures, to act as experts on problems, or to examine the etiology of issues, how they are maintained, and alternatives for solving them is contrary to both CAFT's conceptual framework and what Chinese clients expect from treatment. In addition, their unwillingness to impose their ideas on clients, their lack of acknowledgment that problems exist, and the indirect means by which they encourage the discovery of solutions will give Chinese clients the impression that they are not being helped. And the crystal-ball technique, the cornerstone of the model, is too gimmicky and manipulative, requiring clients to be not only imaginative, but able to recognize that what they are imagining is the solution to their problems. This goes contrary to Chinese pragmatic and linear thought processes. In fact, Chinese clients will find the large amount of time spent elaborating on the miracle as a waste of time.

Nevertheless, although Solution Focused Therapy may not be totally adaptable to working with traditional Chinese families, many aspects of it can be very useful, such as the belief that clients have the resources and skills to find solutions to their problems. The emphasis on wellness, positive connotations, strengths, and change empowers clients, giving them hope that they can overcome the obstacles they face. The genuine admiration and concern demonstrated in treatment allows clients to retain their integrity and self-respect and to feel less ashamed of having to seek outside assistance. As will be demonstrated in subsequent chapters, combining cognitive and behavioral interventions with change, coping, exception, and presuppositional questions is very effective for examining the etiology of problems, their impact on family members, and alternatives for resolving them. Finally, using scaling questions and homework assignments allows clients not only to measure movement, but to feel actively involved and in control of it. This, in turn, serves to reinforce the perception that they and not their therapist are responsible for and in charge of making changes in their life.

Contextual Family Therapy

Contextual Family Therapy, a multigenerational approach to working with families, was developed by Ivan Boszormenyi-Nagy and Geraldine M. Spark (1973). The model is comprehensive and based on four interdependent dimensions: (1) psychology, or the intrapsychic structure of the individual family members; (2) transactions, or power alignments within the family; (3) facts; and (4) relational ethics. The two unique concepts of the model are the last two, which examine issues simply as facts rather than as some form of psychological insecurity and relational ethics.

Facts are issues connected to the actual arrangement of the client's roots and are related to the client's ethnicity, nationality, religion, and characterological and physical traits as well as to family events such as birth, adoption, and illnesses. They are associated with destiny or with circumstances that the individual is powerless to influence or change and may have nothing to do with intrapersonal or interpersonal dynamics. For example, a poor Chinese client with no understanding of English will have limited employment opportunities; a student with severe learning disabilities will have difficulty achieving academically. These issues are concrete realities and should be treated pragmatically: the therapist should help the client to find an English as a Second Language class and the student to find remedial and tutorial services.

The cornerstone of Contextual Family Therapy is the concept of relational ethics. According to Boszormenyi-Nagy and Ulrich (1981, p. 160), it is a "fundamental dynamic force, holding family and societal relationships together through mutuality and trustworthiness of relationship. According to multilateral logic, the balance of fairness between people is the most profound and inclusive context. This is the context to which the term contextual therapy applies."

The basis for relational ethics is inherent and is expressed in family loyalty and the belief that everyone is entitled to have her or his welfare and interests considered in a way that is fair and respectful. These interests or entitlements are inherited and depend on the individual's role and position in the family. Parents, for example, are entitled to be respected and obeyed, whereas their children are entitled to be loved and sheltered.

When fairness or trustworthy relatedness exists between individuals, family members receive what they deserve and loyalty is established. The degree of fairness can be measured on a ledger of merit. Moves toward fairness earn merit points on this ledger and are called *rejunctive*, while moves away from fairness earn no merit points and are called *disjunctive*. A father who physically abuses his son, for example, is in a disjunctive mode and untrustworthy; consequently, he earns no merit points toward having his son be loyal to him. However, even though they may be treated unfairly, children instinctively and unconsciously incur an indebtedness to their parents that requires them to be loyal and give their parents what they are entitled to. The inability to repay this debt creates ethical relatedness; according to Contextual Family Therapy, this is the etiology for emotional and family problems that may be passed on from one generation to the next in the form of legacies.

Family problems derived from unethical relatedness that can be passed on to future generations in the form of legacies are manifested in the following ways:

1. Split loyalty

2. Invisible loyalty

3. Revolving slate

4. Exploitation

5. Interlocking need templates

6. Scapegoating

7. Parentification
8. Rational corruption

In *split loyalty*, children are overtly or covertly encouraged to align themselves with one parent against the other. *Invisible loyalty* refers to the belief that filial loyalty is a universal and central relational dynamic. This dynamic is exploited when parents don't allow their children to demonstrate that loyalty in a functional manner. In the *revolving slate*, dysfunctional family patterns or loyalty issues are passed on from one generation or individual to another. *Exploitation* consists of consciously or unconsciously using someone else to meet one's own personal and psychological needs. With *interlocking need templates*, individuals mutually use one another to meet their own psychological insecurities, whereas *scapegoating* consists of projecting and displacing unethical practices or behaviors onto someone else. In *parentification*, children are overburdened with parental responsibilities. Finally, *relational corruption* is the process of setting up an individual to fail.

Contextual Family Therapy is primarily a cognitive rather than an affective behavioral or interactional approach to treatment. Its overall objective is to translate symptoms into issues of fairness that either encourage or detract from loyalty and then to assist families toward unethical relatedness. Specific goals include (1) confronting invisible loyalties in the family, (2) recognizing unsettled accounts, and (3) rebalancing obligations and relationships with parents and children. These goals are achieved by therapists who provide a safe environment in which clients can explore and understand how the presenting problems are related to issues of fairness and trustworthiness, express their thoughts and feelings regarding personal and family issues, and learn to shift their efforts or intentions in the direction of a rejunctive mode.

Implications for Treatment

Contextual Family Therapy's elicitory approach is not conducive to working with Chinese immigrants, who expect therapy to be problem-centered and prescriptive. However, its concept of relational ethics, which is closely aligned with Confucian philosophy, is very useful as a diagnostic tool. The ideas of entitlement, indebtedness, trustworthiness, legacy, ledger of merit, and rejunctive and disjunctive movement provide a conceptual framework for recognizing ways in which loyalty, the cornerstone of Chinese families, is or is not fostered and maintained. In addition, the eight issues resulting from unethical relatedness provide directions for treatment that can be addressed in a brief therapeutic mode through the use of cognitive, behavioral, structural, strategic, or solution-focused interventions. Finally, Contextual Family Therapy's objective of reciprocal fairness coincides with CAFT's objective of reasonable compromise.

The concept of facts is also very useful in working with Chinese American families because the issues they bring to treatment are often practical rather than intrapersonal or interpersonal. Many clients simply need housing, employment, or language skills. Such issues should not be interpreted to mean something pathological or dysfunctional such as resistance to change, passive aggressive behavior, or an unconscious desire to fail but instead should be accepted at face value and treated pragmatically.

The six treatment approaches described here can be used in conjunction with CAFT to assist clients in resolving problems and in regaining or maintaining the integration of self. Structural Family Therapy's conceptual framework is similar to Chinese families' organizational structure and is ideally suited for working within it to bring about necessary interpersonal compromises. Strategic Therapy is particularly useful for helping therapists who are working indirectly or at a metalevel and for resolving major power struggles. Planned Short-Term Treatment's use of cognitive-behavioral interventions to solve problems matches what Chinese clients expect from therapists, and Rational-Emotive Therapy's cognitive-restructuring approach lends itself to the Chinese analytic and pragmatic style of addressing issues. Several of Solution Focused Therapy's "solution questions" are very useful for empowering clients and helping them to use their own skills and resources to resolve the issues they bring to treatment. Finally, relational ethics, the cornerstone of Contextual Family Therapy, can be used diagnostically to identify problems associated with unethical or untrustworthy relatedness and movement away from loyalty between family members.

These six models provide a therapeutic environment that is warm, respectful, and supportive. With the exception of Solution Focused Therapy and Contextual Family Therapy, they are brief, concrete, problem-oriented, task-centered, active, prescriptive, and focused in the present. Solution Focused Therapy is brief, concrete, task-centered, active, and prescriptive, but it is aimed toward solutions and the future rather than toward problems and the present. Contextual Family Therapy, on the other hand, tends to be open-ended, focused on the past and on understanding while encouraging changes, and elicitory rather than prescriptive. Again, with the exception of Solution Focused Therapy and Contextual Family Therapy, the models perceive the role of the therapist as that of an authority figure, an expert, and a change agent who, among many other interventions, is willing to educate and give advice. Therapists in Solution Focused Therapy view the therapeutic relationship as being egalitarian and the clients as the experts on their problems; consequently, they do not educate or give advice. Therapists in Contextual Family Therapy, on the other hand, consider themselves to be authority figures and experts, but not change agents. Although they may educate, they will not give advice. Instead, they allow clients to make their own discoveries regarding the changes necessary to bring about fairness and harmony in their life.

Now that the theoretical dimensions of CAFT have been articulated, the following two chapters will apply the concepts and principles of practice that have been discussed over the course of treatment. Chapter Five will describe the importance and elements of the initial interview, and Chapter Six will address ongoing treatment and termination.

Chapter Five

First Impressions

Keys to a Successful Start

Using the Lee family as a case example, this chapter describes how to conduct an efficient, effective, and comprehensive first interview with a Chinese American family. The initial interview is critical in establishing a foundation upon which we and our clients can work together to resolve the presenting problems and issues they bring to treatment. To achieve our objectives in therapy, we need to be clear, concise, and orderly in the manner in which we ask clients questions. We also need to know what questions to raise and to whom they should be directed.

The first interview should be two hours in length and divided into the following four stages: (1) socialization, (2) problem, (3) interaction, and (4) closing. The goals in the *socialization* stage are to create a positive and safe atmosphere, acquire knowledge about the characteristics of the family members and observe how they relate to each other, obtain a cursory understanding of the family's current and past relationships, and conduct a cultural assessment. The first three goals are accomplished by joining, making the clients feel comfortable, and obtaining background material such as each person's employment status, interests, and living conditions. The cultural assessment is based on information obtained regarding the clients' place of origin, length of residence in the United States, reasons for immigrating, educational level, socioeconomic status, primary social and civic relationships, languages spoken and food customarily eaten in the home, and primary rituals and traditions observed, as well as any occurrences of interracial or interethnic marriages.

The goals in the *problem stage* are to assist our clients in clearly defining the problems and issues they want to address and then to develop a treatment plan to resolve these problems and issues. This is accomplished by asking each parent about his or her perception of the problems, how long the problems have existed, and what the parent has done in an effort to rectify them. This is followed by having the rest of the family members respond to what has been presented. During the early phase of this stage, we do not want family members to discuss the issues at length; instead, we try to elicit succinct responses. At this point we don't wish to encourage a discussion of issues. Our primary interest is in understanding each family member's view of the issues, discerning the severity of the problems, and determining the level of agreement between the family members, particularly the parents. Once the problems have been clearly assessed, we work with the family to establish a treatment plan.

In the *interaction* stage, we attempt to empower the clients and instill hope by fostering an immediate interactional, behavioral, affective, or attitudinal change. This is normally accomplished by creating an enactment in which some members of the family are engaged in an interaction that has the possibility of leading to a positive outcome. However, this may also be accomplished by encouraging the clients to take action on a particular issue, such as attending a parent education class or enrolling in a job training program.

In the *closing stage*, we review and summarize the session and establish an eight-week contract. Experience has shown that this is generally enough time to effectively address the problems Chinese American clients bring to therapy. If more sessions are necessary, a new contract is negotiated. Unfortunately, many insurance carriers or service providers will not pay their clients for eight sessions. In such instances, we explain what can be accomplished with the limited number of sessions permitted. Generally, the fewer the sessions, the more we are confined to educating the clients, providing information, and referring them to self-help or support groups in the community. In some instances, we refer clients to a counseling agency whose fees are based on a sliding scale.

In this stage, we also describe the regulations and conditions under which treatment will be provided. Included in this discussion are the rules governing confidentiality, paying of fees, and cancellation of appointments. Before ending, we encourage our clients to call if they have any questions between sessions.

Throughout the initial session and subsequent interviews, we highlight issues related to integration, integrity, and Confucian ethical principles, as well as fostering and encouraging movement toward peace and interactional patterns based on reciprocal fairness. We also use our observational skills to see and accurately describe the behavioral data that are presented. This includes identifying the channels of communication and behaviors that are noticed or not noticed by family members; describing the order in which family members speak; noticing nonverbal interactions and the way family members block or facilitate others; and describing circular patterns of interaction, family-therapist interactions, and shifts in interactional patterns. We then use our conceptual skills to translate what we have observed into a diagnosis based on our conceptual framework. Thus, we are always examining and reexamining the therapeutic process and, based on that examination, changing intervention strategies and treatment plans whenever necessary.

Socialization Stage

The Lee family was referred to the Family Service Association of Riverside by the Riverside County Probation Department because George, at age fourteen, had been found guilty of shoplifting with two friends. A condition of his probation was that he and his parents attend counseling. The intake sheet indicated that George lived with his parents, Tom, age forty-six, and Woonie, age forty-three; his sister Patricia, age sixteen; his uncle Raymond, age fifty-three; and his grandmother Nan, age seventy-five. Two other siblings— Susan, age nineteen, and Donald, age twenty-one—went to school at the University of California and lived in Berkeley. The intake sheet also indicated that the family lived in Riverside and owned a small Chinese restaurant and that both parents had a high school education. Attending the first session were George, his parents, and his sister Patricia.

I met the family in the waiting room, introducing myself as Dr. Marshall Jung. I warmly greeted first Mr. Lee and then his wife by shaking their hands to establish physical and emotional contact, making sure I used their surname. I then asked them to introduce their children, whom I greeted by their first name. Before entering the counseling room, I asked if anyone cared for water, tea, or coffee. They politely refused.

Therapy begins the moment you see the family. Often what you observe in the waiting room gives you vital diagnostic information. Once contact has been made, everything we do as therapists should be purposeful. The warm manner in which I welcomed the family was a joining intervention. By calling myself Dr. Jung, I positioned myself as an authority figure, establishing a hierarchical relationship between the parents and me. I then respected and acknowledged the hierarchy between the parents and their children by addressing the parents formally and the children by their first name. The offer of tea and coffee was a gesture of warmth and hospitality. In Chinese homes, you are always welcomed with the offer of something to drink or eat. On a metalevel I was saying to the family, "I know your customs and you are welcome and safe here."

Chairs in the counseling room are arranged in a circle, with family members organizing their own seating arrangement. This allows us to obtain an initial impression of the family's structural arrangements, which include alignments, coalitions, and boundary keeping. The parents sat first, leaving an empty chair between them for Patricia. George pulled his chair out of the circle and slightly away from the rest of the family. He then folded his arms across his chest, indicating to me that he was on the outside of the family unit and closed to any input.

I again respected the family hierarchy by speaking to Mr. Lee first. I told him that before asking questions about why he came to see me (not what brought him to treatment, which is more likely to evoke feelings of shame), I would like to spend a few minutes getting to know the family. I then proceeded to ask questions regarding his business, saying that I hoped it was doing well. I also asked questions that allowed me to do a cultural assessment. Mr. Lee reported that he and his wife had immigrated to this country from Hong Kong seventeen years ago. The two older children were born there and the younger ones were born in the United States. All of them were American citizens. Both Mr. Lee and his wife had worked in restaurants to save enough money to buy their current business, which they purchased ten years ago. Now he was thinking of selling it because business had seriously deteriorated as a result of increased crime and gang violence in the neighborhood. However, this was going to be a difficult decision because neither he nor his wife wished to go back to working for others.

During the course of the conversation, I attempted to join with him by indicating that he resembled my father, who also worked hard at a small business so that his children could have a better life. I tried to make a bridge between him and George by asking George if he knew that one of the reasons his father worked so hard was that he wanted George to be successful. George only responded by saying, "I guess so." I told George that it was true and that Chinese parents showed their love and concern for their children by their hard work. I then turned to Mrs. Lee to obtain affirmation of what I had said. She agreed. This was a positive-connotation intervention, not only highlighting the parents' hard work and positive intentions but also conveying to George that his parents cared about his well-being.

I joined with Mrs. Lee by saying that she must be proud of having two children attending a major university. I also told her that I had two children, one of whom was living in Hong Kong, who were also doing well. I then obtained more background information. She said that she and her husband had little time for socializing with the few friends they had in the Los Angeles area because of the long hours they put into their business. The extent of their entertainment was watching Chinese television shows. Occasionally, their older children forced them to take short vacation trips to

San Francisco. My last request of Mrs. Lee before moving on to Patricia was to describe the positive things about her children. This was another effort to highlight the positive attributes of the family before addressing their problems. She didn't say much, but it was obvious that she was proud of them. I ended my conversation with her by saying that it must bring her peace to know that she had children who were hard-working, responsible, and respectful.

I next chatted with Patricia about her interests and how she liked school. I also asked her to describe her perception of the family dynamics. She indicated that with the exception of George, they all got along well. It wasn't that they had conflicts with him; he simply wasn't around. They all helped in the restaurant (Susan and Donald returned to help during summer breaks) while George was out with his friends. Patricia said she believed that George was only close to his grandmother, who favored and spoiled him. She also said that everyone in the home spoke Chinese except George, who knew how to but in the last two years had refused to do so except with his grandmother.

As with Patricia, I began with George by asking him what he enjoyed doing. He said he enjoyed hanging out with his friends, going to movies, and riding his bike. I tried to pursue his interest in movies and the activities of his friends but only received short responses. I then asked how he was doing in school. He said that he was doing okay but would not elaborate. By his responses to my inquiries, my observation at the beginning of the session that George was closed to any input was substantiated. Rather than continuing to intrude on him by my questioning, I asked him if he felt that he had been forced into seeing me. He said yes. I tried again to join with him by saying that I was sorry he didn't feel the need for counseling but I hoped he might change later, because he didn't seem happy or at peace. I then tried to connect all the family members by saying that it must be difficult for everyone to see a stranger regarding personal matters.

My initial impression of the family was that it was high-functioning, with responsible, intelligent, and caring parents and three successful children. I thought that George was intelligent, sensitive, and angry. Although he appeared to be closed to any input, he responded to me in a respectful and polite manner, indicating that if I approached him with kindness and support, he would allow himself to trust me. It was evident that the parents were very traditional; they spoke primarily Chinese, watched Chinese entertainment, and had primarily Chinese friends. With the exception of George, Mr. and Mrs. Lee had a good relationship with their children. There appeared to be rigid boundary keeping between George and his parents and siblings. Finally, based on Patricia's comments, I thought that George and his grandmother might have a special relationship. I felt that with the exception of George, I had joined well with the family members and they felt comfortable with me. And, although George was distrustful, I thought I could eventually join with him.

The socialization phase of the interview continued for nearly thirteen minutes, ending when I thanked the family members for sharing something about themselves with me. I then entered the problem stage of the session by asking the parents to describe the concerns that had brought them to see me.

Problem Stage

I began the problem stage of the interview by asking Mr. and Mrs. Lee what had brought them to treatment. They said that in addition to George's shoplifting, they were having several other problems with him, including talking back, staying out late, associating with "bad" kids, stealing money and then lying about it, refusing to help in the restaurant or at home, using bad language (profanity and street talk), missing school, and performing poorly in school. The following week the parents were scheduled to meet with school representatives, who were considering suspension. They agreed that the problems started about the time George entered middle school and began associating with "bad" kids. At the mention of his friends, George gave a disgusted look and stated under his breath that his father "doesn't know what the fuck he's talking about." Mr. Lee reacted to this statement by angrily telling George that he wasn't any good. I immediately moved in to defuse and normalize the angry feelings and conflict by telling Mr. Lee that I would also be upset if my son talked to me in such a disrespectful manner and telling George that I felt sorry he believed his father didn't understand him. By making supportive comments to both, I joined with each and maintained my neutrality.

This disruptive episode was very important to treatment. First, it broke the formality in the session and allowed me to observe the way conflict was manifested at home. Second, it allowed me to observe one set of behaviors that triggered and reinforced the conflict between George and his father. Mr. Lee criticized George's friends; George, in turn, attacked his father, who in turn counterattacked him. Both were in a reactive mode, neither hearing nor caring about the other person's thoughts or feelings. Third, it allowed me to demonstrate my concern for both of them. Fourth, my intervention demonstrated that I was in control of the session and would not permit destructive interactions. Finally, my intervention organized the problem between George and his father in a constructive rather than a destructive framework. I indicated to Mr. Lee that George did not demonstrate respect and to George that his father did not demonstrate understanding. I implied that George wanted understanding while his father wanted respect. This would be incorporated into the treatment plan later, as I helped them to obtain what they wanted and thus helped to bring about peace between them.

I continued the interview by asking the parents what they believed were the causal factors for the problems and what they had tried to do to rectify them. They said that George was "not like their other children, but lazy." Patricia concurred with her parents, adding that she also thought his problems were associated with being spoiled by his grandmother. The parents had tried corporal punishment, but they now thought he was too old for such consequences. They had tried withholding things from him, but his grandmother had undermined them by continuing to give him money and buying things he wanted. Now they felt helpless to do anything but yell and complain.

Later in the session, I said to the parents that it must be difficult for them at times to find peace with a son who was causing them so many problems. I then asked them what it was like before George entered middle school. They said that he had been a "good" boy, helpful, obedient, and easy to get along with. I said that I hoped it would be like that again. I then asked George what getting along with everyone had been like. He simply replied, "It was all right." In this sequence I reintroduced the theme of peace. I also tried to instill hope and create a more positive atmosphere before discussing the problem issues with George. Next, I asked George to respond to what his parents had said about the concerns they had for him. In this way, I reinforced the hierarchy in the family. If I had asked for his perception of the problems, it would have put him on the same level as his parents.

With my support and encouragement to share his thoughts, George said that his parents were rigid, "old-fashioned," and too strict. He believed that they wanted him to be like his siblings, whom he considered to be "straight." He saw himself as different from them, fun-loving, outgoing, and sociable, and felt that this was unacceptable to his parents, who constantly emphasized study, responsibility, and obedience. He thought that no one, including his grandmother, understood or accepted him, and with the exception of his grandmother, no one cared for him or provided him with support. All he wanted was to be left alone.

My diagnostic impressions were that George's problems began when he entered early adolescence and were due, in part, to his search for identity and his and his parents' inability to negotiate their differences in family and cultural expectations. His parents wanted him, like the three other children, to adhere to Chinese values by organizing his time around academic achievement and being with and supporting the family and its business. He rebelled against their expectations by doing poorly in school, not helping in the business, associating with peers they disapproved of, shoplifting, and emphasizing that he wanted to be "different" and "alone" rather than being the same and part of the family. In so doing, he attacked the family values of respectfulness, responsibility, loyalty, and honesty. As a result, rigid boundaries were established between him and his parents and siblings with interactional patterns and behaviors that continued to reinforce movement away from integration and interpersonal compromise.

I asked Mr. Lee to select two problems from the list of problems he had named, the two he thought were most important and would like to address first. He replied that he wanted George to attend and do well in school and to stop talking back. For the next several minutes I pursued the issue of why he thought it was important for George to do well in school. He explained the many reasons why an education would be helpful to his son. Following my discussion with Mr. Lee, I turned to George and asked if he knew how concerned his father was about his future. He said that all his father did was yell and scream at him. I responded by saying that although that might be true, it appeared to me that he was doing it because he wanted George to have a successful future. I then asked what it was like knowing his father wanted him to do well. George did not answer but sat quietly. I let a few minutes of silence pass to let the idea of his father wanting something positive for him sink in and then told George that he should think more about the fact that his father wanted him to do well. This was another effort to get George to recognize and accept that his father actually cared for him.

In this sequence, I drew out and amplified Mr. Lee's concern about George's future well-being. In doing so I directed the session away from a negative atmosphere of criticism and condemnation and toward a positive one by helping George to recognize that his father meant well and was concerned about him. At this point, it would be difficult for George to acknowledge his father's concern, and therefore it was not important that he respond to my question; what was important was that he recognize his father's concern. If he made this perceptual shift, his negative feelings toward his parents would change to positive ones and would be reflected in positive behavior.

I then asked the parents if I could attend the meeting with them at the school. I explained that I would treat the meeting as part of therapy and that they would be billed only for the time I actually spent at the school. I went on to explain why I thought it was important, including the fact that a plan of action for getting George to attend and do well in school would need to be based on information from that meeting, as well as on obtaining support and cooperation from George's teachers. Mr. and Mrs. Lee initially resisted, saying that it would be too much trouble for me. This is a typical response given out of politeness. I answered that it was something I wanted to do and again reiterated its importance. They then gratefully accepted my offer. I wanted to address the problem of George's talking back in the next stage of treatment.

Attending school meetings with parents is important for many reasons. First, because of the time and effort involved in going to the school, it demonstrates to the family a genuine concern for them. Second, for Chinese families, it incurs a debt, which they wish to repay. Repayment is often made by giving a small gift or food. These gifts are also a gesture of appreciation. Third, the information regarding academic performance, classroom behavior, and the client's relationship with teachers and peers is very important for assessment and treatment. Finally, schoolteachers and officials are more likely to support and cooperate with families in establishing a plan of correction when a therapist is involved and in attendance.

Once I had defined the treatment goals, I turned my attention to addressing the problem of George's talking back. Knowing that he still was angry at his father, I decided to address this issue by having George speak with his mother in the next stage of the interview.

Interaction Stage

In the interaction stage of the interview, I hoped to use the issue of talking back as a way to engage George and his mother in a positive exchange. To foster a conversation, I asked George to move close to, and in front of, his mother. He complied. By so doing I created a subgroup to intensify the interaction that was to follow. I then asked George what he wanted from his parents. This served four purposes. First, it modeled for the parents a different way of engaging their son. Next, it sent a message to George that I was not like his parents, who only told him what they wanted. In addition, it said to George that I was concerned about his needs. And finally, it gave George an opportunity to state his concerns. He said nothing and reiterated that he just wanted to be left alone. I challenged him by stating that I didn't believe him and that based on his former statements, I felt he wanted to be understood and cared for. I didn't expect or push for an acknowledgment. I merely wanted to join with him by conveying that I knew some of his needs.

I asked Mrs. Lee to explain to George why it was important that he speak to her in a respectful manner. Following her brief explanation, I asked George if he had any questions or comments. I was again modeling for the parents and sending the message to George that I was interested in his thoughts. He shook his head, implying no. I then briefly explained to George that his parents wanted him to be respectful because they wanted him to possess this positive attribute. I then thanked him for talking with me in a respectful manner.

The objective in this sequence was to again build on the parents' positive intentions, highlight the importance of respect, and convey to George that his parents cared for him and were concerned about his well-being.

Closing Stage

In this stage, I pointed out the many positive things I saw in the family and then briefly explained why I thought George had so many problems. I highlighted the fact that I knew his parents wanted the best for him but said that at the moment he couldn't see it. I again told George that his parents wanted the best for him and that he should think about that thought. I also asked him to consider the issues he would like to discuss with his parents for our next session. I explained to the family that we would continue with the school-related problems and George's disrespectful conduct before moving on to the other presenting problems. Thus, I followed the principle of keeping things manageable by working on only a few issues. I requested and received permission to talk with the referring probation officer to learn firsthand the conditions of probation and what was expected from family therapy. This information could be valuable in treatment. I established an eight-week contract for treatment and explained to the family the policies regarding cancellations, payment of fees, and confidentiality.

Near the end of the session, I asked Mr. Lee if he had considered contacting the small business bureau and trying to obtain a minority business loan to move his business into a safer and more prosperous neighborhood. He said that he was not aware of such loans. I told him that if he wished, I could find the telephone number of someone to contact. He said he would think about it. I also suggested that if Mr. and Mrs. Lee decided to close the restaurant, before doing so they could receive job training in another area of interest. This would prepare them to find a job other than in a restaurant. I told them that if they wished, I could give them the telephone number of a job training program that helped Chinese Americans in Los Angeles. Mr. Lee thanked me and said he would think about it.

This sequence allowed me to join with Mr. Lee by giving him some practical suggestions and by letting him know that I could be a resource person for him. It also demonstrated my concern for the couple.

I thought that Nan's involvement in the family was significant to the case and therefore requested her presence. However, the couple politely refused my request by saying that she wasn't feeling well.

My major themes throughout the session were to join with George, model for Mr. and Mrs. Lee a better way to engage their son, create an atmosphere in which George would feel understood, highlight the importance of respect in Chinese families, and instill in George's mind the fact that his parents genuinely cared for him. I believed that if George could recognize his parents' concern, he would begin to respond to them in a respectful, honest, responsible, and loyal manner, and that they in turn would be willing to acquiesce to some of his requests and needs.

I addressed directly and pragmatically the parents' major concern, George's attendance at school, by asking to go with the parents to meet with school personnel. I also established a collaborative relationship with Mr. and Mrs. Lee and a treatment direction they agreed upon.

In Chapter Six, I will describe the clinical process over the next six sessions, beginning with the school visit.

Chapter Six

Treatment and Termination

The clinical process should be linear and continuous, with each session building on the previous one. To accomplish this objective, it is important to stay focused on the presenting problems and the goals established in the initial session. In this case, the two major problems the Lee family chose to address first were George's problems in school and his disrespectful behavior.

In addition to the presenting problems, therapists using CAFT select themes or issues that reinforce the problems they are focusing on. The themes are based on our clinical assessment and the needs of our clients. They may be used for one session or throughout the therapeutic process. In the case of the Lee family, George did not feel understood or liked and therefore a theme throughout treatment was to convey the opposite.

Course of Treatment

Prior to our second meeting, I contacted Mr. Ramos, George's probation officer. He informed me that George had to continue in therapy until I felt that treatment was no longer needed. George also could not associate with the two friends with whom he had shoplifted and had to be home by 9:00 every evening. I asked that George attend school regularly as a condition of probation. Mr. Ramos's support would empower Mr. and Mrs. Lee, giving them someone to turn to if George did not attend school.

Second Session: School Meeting

Attending the school meeting were Mrs. Lee (her husband had to be at the restaurant), the boys' vice principal, the school counselor, and George's mathematics, English, and history teachers. They all showed genuine concern for George and were willing to work with him to keep him in school and improve his grades. Academically, he was receiving grades of D+ and C–, but he could improve his grades if he attended classes and turned in assignments. They all agreed that he could be working at an A or B grade level. They also agreed that he was withdrawn, but respectful and compliant when given instructions. Socially, he was shy but was liked by his peers. His major problem at school was his many unexcused absences, which would lead to suspension if they continued.

Throughout the meeting, I worked at conveying to George the concern people had for his well-being and emphasized that if he would allow his teachers, they would help him to raise his grades. I asked what it was like for him to know that Ms. Chow, his English teacher, hoped he would do well because he was a nice young man. He responded by saying, "I don't know," but I sensed that he appreciated the concern. I also highlighted, especially to his mother, his ability to be respectful and the fact that he was well liked. This was a cognitive restructuring effort to change Mrs. Lee's perception of him from a son who was considered bad to one who demonstrated respect and had a great deal of potential.

My role in the meeting was that of mediator. I encouraged George to give his input as to what would work best for him. In doing so, I was sending him the message that people wanted to understand him and that I thought what he said was important. I also supported Mrs. Lee's authority by making sure that everything in the plan met with her approval. During the first week, George would meet with each teacher, who would devise a plan for him to improve his grades. Every Friday George would bring home a report, signed by each of his teachers, testifying that he was doing his assigned work. Finally, the school agreed to call George's parents any day he was not in school.

Working with the school to support Mr. and Mrs. Lee and to devise a plan to help George remain in school was a systems intervention. With the aid of the school and the probation department, the parents gained the support they needed to reassert their authority over their son.

Third Session

Present in the third session were Mrs. and Mrs. Lee and George. The meeting began with Mrs. Lee giving me a box of tea and mooncakes. It was the couple's way of joining with me and expressing gratitude for my help. I thanked them and accepted their gift, because it would have been impolite not to.

Before asking how things were going with George, I asked Mr. Lee if he had any questions regarding our meeting with the school, to which he replied that his wife had explained everything. I shared with them my discussion with Mr. Ramos and the fact that George's school attendance was now part of the conditions for probation. I didn't tell them that it was my idea for fear of alienating George. I then asked them if they would call Mr. Ramos if George missed school, to which they replied yes. I asked Mr. Lee to tell George directly what he would do if George did not attend school. This sequence empowered the parents, who until then felt they had no way of backing up their demand that he attend school. It also made clear to George the consequences of any disobedience. I then joined with George by telling him that I did not tell the school he was on probation, in order to protect his privacy and to protect him from being labeled a delinquent adolescent. I asked him if he wanted me to protect his privacy, to which he replied yes.

In the next segment of the session, I asked the parents how things were going at home. They said that things were a little better. George was attending school, turning in assignments, and remaining home, aloof but not disrespectful. I then used a solution-focused intervention by asking family members to respond to the question, "How did that happen?" Both parents said that they didn't know but had decided to make no requests of him and to leave him alone. I told George that it looked as though his parents were respecting his right to privacy and asked him to describe what it was like to have his request respected. He said that it was all right. I then asked George how it happened that he was being respectful. He said that he didn't know. I didn't expect George to describe what had happened; I was just highlighting the change in his behavior. I closed this segment by telling the parents that they had found part of the solution to their problem by respecting George's privacy. This intervention gave credit to the parents for the change and acknowledged that they had the insight to find their own solutions to their problems.

In this segment, it is clear that a small change had taken place. George was not really engaged in the family but, more importantly at this time, he was not creating any problems. I tried to build on this small change with more solution-focused interventions. I also built on the theme of respect I had begun at the beginning of treatment. I continued to build on the positives and the theme of family harmony in the next segment by using another solution-focused intervention. During the next seven to ten minutes I had the family amplify on what it had been like to live this past week in a peaceful home. Following this segment, I asked to speak to George alone. This allowed me to join further with him and create an environment in which he felt less threatened and was more likely to speak. In addition, because Chinese parents expect therapists to talk with the problem child, seeing George alone accorded with what they expected from treatment.

In my discussion with George, I used reflective listening skills to draw him out and have him describe his thoughts and feelings. The content of the discussion was not as important as making George feel supported and understood. During this segment I was careful not to side with George against his parents, but to help him find a way to convey his issues in a constructive manner. Only in this way could he foster a compromise with his parents and thereby find peace within himself. During this segment, I was able to help George describe more clearly the unfairness and cultural differences he experienced at home. I told him that I was willing to help him present these issues to his parents but that he must continue to go to school and not create any disruption at home; otherwise his parents would justifiably become angry and closed to any discussion. This was a cognitive intervention called "logical conclusion." George agreed to continue in school and not create any problems as long as his parents continued to leave him alone. I closed the segment by giving George the homework task of listing ten things he would like from his parents.

In the closing segment, I summarized the session and highlighted the changes that had taken place, particularly the fact that George was going to school and behaving respectfully. I then encouraged the parents to continue doing what they were doing, especially leaving their son alone. I shared with them that George would like to discuss certain things with them the following week. This began to prepare them for the next session by encouraging them to think about what he might say and how they might respond. I closed the session by asking if they had any questions.

Fourth Session

It was obvious at the beginning of the fourth session that there had been a setback. The evening before, George had come home late and drunk. His father had spoken to him angrily and sent him to his room. I asked the parents if they had reported him to Mr. Ramos. They said that they hadn't because they had wanted my advice first. This was a sign that they respected my authority and judgment.

Before sharing my thoughts, I asked how George had behaved the rest of the week. They indicated that his behavior was the same as it had been the week before. He was attending school, turning in his assignments, and being aloof but respectful at home. I asked them what having another peaceful week, with the exception of last evening, had been like. Before I asked to see George alone, we spent a few minutes talking about the peace they had enjoyed.

It did not surprise me that George had misbehaved in a manner that would provoke a response from his parents. He was accustomed to living in a home in which there was conflict between him and his parents. I suspected that the peace between them, coupled with having to share his thoughts with his parents in treatment, had created too much anxiety for him. To relieve that anxiety, avoid sharing his thoughts with his parents, and return to a homeostatic state that was familiar, albeit dysfunctional, he unconsciously misbehaved. I think he also was testing me to see whether or not I would continue to be supportive and respectful of him even if he acted out.

I entered my discussion with George with the goal of continuing to be supportive, understanding, and accepting. I asked him what had made him get drunk and stay out late. He said he didn't know. I then made a presuppositional statement and said that he must feel disappointed in not being able to continue to do well. This statement implied that he did intend to do well. Before he could respond, I said that everyone slips and makes mistakes, but that he couldn't blame his parents for being disappointed and angry. Again, I used the cognitive intervention called logical conclusion, which postulates that certain behaviors will elicit natural responses. In this case, George's parents would inherently be upset with him any time he misbehaved. I also said that based on his previous behaviors, his parents had learned not to trust him. I was laying the groundwork for the theme of trust. We spent the next several minutes discussing what trust meant to him and what role it played in his relationship with his friends. During the conversation I asked him if he had done his homework assignment, to which he said no.

I then asked if he wanted a trusting relationship with his parents and if he wanted to discuss his concerns with them. After much discussion, he answered yes to both questions. I said that we would try to talk with his parents again the following week. In the meantime, he was to try to stay out of trouble and do his homework assignment. Before ending this segment, however, I shared with

George my belief that he was unconsciously getting into trouble because he was afraid to talk with his parents. I went on to explain why I believed this was true. He did not agree. I closed by stating my reasons, and I predicted that he would unconsciously misbehave again. Sharing my thoughts about why he misbehaved and predicting that it would happen again were not intended to give George any insight into his motives. They were a strategic intervention. By predicting failure based on the reasons I had given, I put George in a positive paradoxical situation. If he failed I would be right and we could openly address his fears about speaking with his parents. If he proved me wrong, he would continue to behave and I could work with him and his parents in a calm rather than a hostile climate.

Following my talk with George, I met with him and his parents. I suggested that they give George a chance and not report his misconduct to Mr. Ramos. My recommendation was based on the fact that for nearly two weeks, George had been doing well. I then highlighted the positive changes. When they agreed to give him another chance, I highlighted this forgiving gesture. I closed the session by reiterating to George that his parents wanted him to do well.

This session could have easily gotten bogged down in George's misbehavior. However, I avoided a no-win confrontation over why he came home late and drunk by seeing George alone and not discussing the issue. I continued to support George, highlight the positives, and stay focused on the goal of having George engage his parents in a constructive conversation. I introduced the theme of trust, which I would use in subsequent sessions. Finally, I was able to take a negative incident, that of George coming home late and drunk, and turn it into a positive outcome, that of his parents demonstrating care by not reporting him to Mr. Ramos.

Fifth Session

The family canceled their next appointment because Mrs. Lee was ill; therefore, the fifth session was held a week later. After chatting about their restaurant business, I asked the parents how George was doing. They said that he was continuing to attend school regularly, turn in assignments, and remain at home without creating any prob-lems. I again used a solution-focused question and asked how this had happened. They said that they still tried not to bother him even though they felt he should help in the restaurant. George, in turn, said that they were leaving him alone. He spent most of his time listening to music and watching television. I asked George if his grades were improving, to which he replied that he was earning C's instead of D's. I told him that was an improvement and showed effort on his part. I also acknowledged that he was right about not being afraid to talk to his parents. I then ask if he had completed the assignment. He said that he could name only four things he wanted out of the ten I'd asked for.

Before asking George to speak with his parents, I reiterated what I had said to them in the first session about why I thought George had so many problems. I then explained the difficulty ado-lescents have in integrating two cultures. After some discussion, the parents agreed with my assessment. I asked them if they would be willing to hear what George had to say. They said yes. By asking their permission, I acknowledged their authority.

With my support, George presented his four requests. He wanted to be able to socialize with his friends, to be given an allowance, to dress the way he wished, and to have his ear pierced. Knowing that his parents were not accustomed to exploring their children's thoughts, I took the initiative and spent the next several minutes talking about the reasons behind these requests. This modeled for the parents how to effectively engage their son. I then asked the parents if their son was making himself clear, to which they said he was. I asked if they had any questions, and they said they didn't. They immediately denied his request to pierce his ear, because they believed that wearing earrings was only for girls. I explained to George that understanding an issue doesn't necessary mean agree-ing with it. Mr. and Mrs. Lee said that they would think about the other three requests and let him know what they had decided the following week. I asked George if he felt that his parents understood the reasons behind his requests, and he said yes.

I believe this was the turning point in treatment. For the first time, George acknowledged that he was understood, which also implied that he was heard. I also felt that he finally accepted the message that his parents cared and were concerned about his well-being. With this understanding, he would reciprocate by behaving and being respectful.

In the next segment of the session, Mr. and Mrs. Lee discussed the importance of honesty and trust with George. I talked about the importance of living by Confucian ethical principles, even in this country. The couple concurred. I then explained to George how I thought his parents adhered to these principles. This allowed me to continue highlighting the parents' strengths and to convey to George how Chinese parents demonstrate care and support.

Sixth and Seventh Sessions

In the sixth session, the parents reported that George continued to go to school and remained out of trouble. They agreed that as long as he continued to behave, he could socialize with his friends, within limits. They also agreed that he could choose his own clothes, within limits, and agreed to give him an allowance. I used the next fifteen to twenty minutes teaching the family the communication skills they needed to discuss the rules governing George's participation with his friends and his selection of clothes.

With the family communicating constructively, the last half of the session and all of the next session were devoted to successfully negotiating Mr. and Mrs. Lee's expectations regarding George's responsibilities at home. By the end of the seventh session, it was apparent that the problems that had brought the family to treatment had been resolved. George felt understood and supported by his parents, talked with them in a respectful manner, improved his grades at school, and helped at home. Mr. and Mrs. Lee were satisfied with George's behavior and believed they could trust him with his friends. As a result, we agreed to terminate treatment in the next session.

Termination Session

Termination can be as important as the other sessions, if not more important. If it is not planned or conducted properly, the gains made in treatment may not be stabilized or anchored. In some instances, they may even be reversed. To ensure a good discharge, therapists must remember, more than at any other time in treatment, the nature of the professional relationship we have with our clients. It is formed for a recognized and agreed-upon purpose, carries authority, and is controlled. Furthermore, it is for the benefit of the client and is time-bound. Therapists, particularly those who are experienced, keep sight of these last two factors.

Sometimes we take a special liking to some of our clients and want to continue the relationship following treatment. More often, however, it is the reverse, with clients wanting to turn the professional relationship into a friendship. In either case, it is not only unethical to do so but can be emotionally damaging to our clients and negate the gains made in therapy. The desire to continue the relationship is normally a reflection of transference on the part of our clients and countertransference on our part.

In some circumstances, clients establish a genuine fondness for us and wish to continue the relationship by exchanging holiday cards or gifts or writing letters. In other instances, they wish to continue the relationship because they have difficulty with separation issues. In either case, we must end the relationship when treatment is completed. In doing so, we may be required to address issues related to loss and separation as part of the treatment process.

As in the case of the Lee family, treatment should end when the presenting problems are resolved. This may take fewer than eight sessions. Chinese families are generally grateful for termination when their problems are resolved. Although it is useful, therapy is an intrusion on their daily routine. Like most of us, they simply wish to get on with their life.

Therapists using CAFT should always strive to end treatment formally, preferably with a termination session. However, this is not always possible. Some clients withdraw from therapy prematurely without informing us and before the presenting problems have been resolved; others believe that a formal ending is not required. With the former, we contact the clients either by phone or in writing to learn why they have stopped attending and, if the problems still persist, to invite them back. If they continue to reject our assistance, we respect their decision, thank them for coming, wish them well, and indicate that they are welcome to return anytime in the future. This procedure acknowledges the clients' right to self-determination, ends our relationship on a positive and supportive note, and makes it safe for them to return to treatment if they change their mind.

The beliefs of those who do not wish a termination session are also respected. We don't try to impose a formal ending session. Instead, as part of the final session, we ask our clients to briefly go over what they have gained from treatment, summarize our observations, invite the clients to return if they ever need services, and wish them well.

For therapists using CAFT, the objectives of the termination session are to clarify any remaining questions, anchor or solidify the changes that occurred in treatment, and have a warm ending. This is accomplished by adhering to the following guidelines:

1. Allow sufficient time to ensure a closing session. For any number of reasons, clients may need to cancel the final session. Consequently, for therapists, students, or interns leaving the agency, the ending session should be scheduled at least three weeks before terminating.

2. Prepare clients for the last meeting by describing its purpose and objectives and having them think about two or three things they have gained or learned from the treatment process.

3. Toward the beginning of the session, ask if they have any final questions that need to be addressed.

4. Ask each member of the family to summarize what he or she has received or learned from treatment.

5. Summarize what has happened in treatment, describing the changes that have been made, how they came about, and the strengths of the family and each of its members.

6. Give credit to the family members for achieving the treatment goals. Before ending, reiterate the importance of maintaining family loyalty and harmony.

7. Have refreshments such as tea, oranges, or fortune cookies available in the session. Chinese socialize over food; therefore, serving refreshments is a nice and warm way to say good-bye.

8. Shortly before ending the session, socialize with the family while retaining the formality of the relationship.

9. Accept any small and inexpensive gifts that may be given.

10. Wish the clients well.

Termination with the Lee Family

Patricia asked to attend our last meeting because she was interested in becoming a psychologist and wanted information from me regarding opportunities in the field, courses of study, and the names of universities with good programs. I welcomed her and the rest of the family into the counseling room, where the seats were again arranged in a circle. Unlike the first meeting, George remained in the circle, indicating that the rigid boundary that had existed between him and his parents had been removed. However, it was evident from his facial expressions and body language that he was disturbed. Before addressing that disturbance, I answered Patricia's questions, while again praising Mr. and Mrs. Lee for having such ambitious children.

After answering Patricia's questions, I asked her how the family was doing. She said that things appeared to be much better and that George was even coming to her for help with his studies. I then turned to George, commending him for his change in attitude toward school and his willingness to reach out for help. To amplify that change and instill a feeling of pride, I asked him the solution-focused question, "How did that happen?" followed by "What is it like doing well in school?"

I then turned my attention to the parents, asking them how things were at home. Mr. Lee said that they were fine, but that George was upset because he was not being allowed to stay overnight with some friends the upcoming weekend. I asked George if he had explained to his parents the reasons he wanted to be with his friends and he said yes. I then asked if he believed that his parents understood his reasoning. He again said yes but went on to state that they refused to change their mind. Mr. Lee said that he was afraid George might get into trouble again. I supported his authority and decision by telling George that not enough time had elapsed for his parents to trust him fully under those circumstances. I went on to say that their decision was made out of concern for him. I then joined and supported George's feelings by telling his parents that it was normal for him to feel unhappy and disappointed; after all, he wasn't being allowed to be with his friends.

What was significant and a good indication that George's attitude and behavior had changed significantly was the fact that he did not misbehave or show hostility toward his father for rejecting his request. His feelings of disappointment were normal and appropriate.

I offered hope to George by saying that if his behavior continued to improve, his parents might consider granting such a request later. I then asked if he wished to discuss the issue further with his parents. He said no. I congratulated him for remaining in control of his behavior, even in the face of disappointment, and indicated to him that he was demonstrating maturity. This sequence served two purposes. It highlighted and rewarded George's self-control. It also served to indirectly educate his parents. I then turned to his parents and asked what it was like knowing that their son was maturing, and they went on to discuss the ways in which they found it good. This sequence helped the parents to recognize and validate George's growth.

Continuing to respect the family hierarchy, I returned to my agenda and asked the parents if they had any unanswered questions or issues they would like to discuss. They said no. I then asked George the same question. He also said no. Moving on, I asked the parents to describe what they would be taking away from therapy. They briefly described the fact that they were pleased with the changes that had taken place and said that thanks to my help, George continued to do well in school and be respectful at home. I acknowledged my role as guide but emphasized that it was they, and not I, who had brought about the changes. To support my statements, I pointed out that George began to change when they decided to respect his desire to be left alone.

I then asked George what he had learned from therapy. He said that he now understood how his parents demonstrated concern for him and he now felt part of the family. I shared with him my belief that he had matured in a short period of time and highlighted the many changes he had made, particularly in learning to be respectful to his parents. In the previous session, I had asked his mother to bring in George's latest report from school. I read aloud the comments made by his teachers; they helped to highlight and reinforce the positive changes he had made.

I then briefly summarized the entire treatment process, highlighting the changes and giving the family credit for them. I also read to the family a summary treatment report I was sending to Mr. Ramos. I asked if they had any questions about or disagreements with any of my clinical observations. There were no questions or disagreements. The family knew that Mr. Ramos wanted a report on the treatment for his records and they had signed a release-of-information form. It is standard practice for therapists using CAFT to share with our clients any report we write that leaves the agency. The clients are also given the opportunity to ask any questions they may have about the report.

Toward the end of the session, I briefly socialized with the family, discussing current events and social issues. I again accepted the parents' gift of tea and mooncakes. They invited Rosie and me to dinner at their restaurant, but I politely refused by saying that agency policy would not permit it. I closed the session by inviting them to return if they needed any further assistance.

This case demonstrated the use of CAFT with the Lee family, which had been upset and fragmented because of the intergenerational conflict between fourteen-year-old George and his parents. George's presenting problems were oppositional behavior at home, poor school performance, and delinquent behavior. Mr. and Mrs. Lee believed that George was disrespectful, lazy, and dishonest. George believed that his parents were unreasonable, didn't understand him, and weren't concerned about his well-being. Through the use of a variety of interventions, I was able to help the family to resolve its intergenerational differences and achieve family integration by helping George to recognize that his parents understood his needs and were concerned about him, and by helping his parents make compromises to meet some of their son's needs. By the end of treatment, George was behaving respectfully, responsibly, and honestly; in turn, his parents provided him with the support he wanted and needed.

Chapter Seven

"I Want to Live"

The Woo Family and Family Integration

Chapter Seven begins to demonstrate the application of CAFT with different families. The five case examples in Chapters Seven through Eleven represent a range of presenting problems, including chronic depression and suicidal ideation, marital conflict, child abuse, schizophrenia, and intergenerational conflict. They will be used to illustrate how CAFT's theoretical concepts, principles of practice, and interventions are used to help individuals and families in treatment, resolve their problems, and achieve family integration.

This chapter tells the story of John Woo, a chronically depressed and suicidal first-generation Chinese American. The case was complicated by the fact that John had already received a year of unsuccessful treatment by another therapist and commuted nearly an hour and a half to see me. I hope that this case shows how to overcome such complications, effectively engage parents who are unwilling to attend treatment, and use creative clinical interventions.

John was a thirty-nine-year-old first-generation Chinese American, referred to me by Mr. Kahle, his therapist of nearly a year. The treatment focus with John and Mr. Kahle was on individuation, the process by which we become ourselves, indivisible and distinct from other people. Initially, John's parents had been involved in the sessions, with a twofold objective: first, to persuade Mr. and Mrs. Woo to recognize and accept the negative influence they may have had on their son's life, and second, to provide him with emotional support by verbalizing feelings of care and concern. However, according to John, his parents would neither accept any responsibility for his problems nor verbalize any nurturing statements. They believed that they had provided a good home environment and that John's problems were caused by his dismissal from work, unemployment, and failed marriage. The couple eventually withdrew from therapy, agreeing to participate only by telephone. Mr. Kahle continued to work in vain, trying to help John to disengage from his parents and move on with his life.

In reviewing the case, it was evident that John's unsuccessful treatment was due, in part, to Mr. Kahle's lack of familiarity with the Chinese American culture. Consequently, treatment had been limited to focusing only on John's American perspective and did not take into consideration the values and norms internalized from his Chinese American upbringing. His inability to see John in his complete cultural context limited Mr. Kahle's clinical options as well as prevented him from knowing how to elicit support from John's parents, whose views were embedded in Chinese rather than Western culture.

Initial Interview

In the initial session, John appeared very anxious, depressed, overwhelmed, and sad. After some polite conversation, he said that he was referred to me because I was recognized as a specialist in working with Chinese families. His statement implied his recognition of me as an expert and authority figure. I immediately asked how he was feeling. I felt able to ask him an affective question because I perceived that he was sensitive to and familiar with addressing emotions as a result of his work with Mr. Kahle. He said, as he normally did, that he was depressed and wanted to kill himself. I didn't want to discuss his problems at once, so after joining by conveying sympathy for his feelings, I proceeded to socialize while gathering background information.

John lived alone in a studio apartment in Orange County, California. He was an unemployed social worker living on state disability and money given to him by his long-term woman friend, Jan. He had previously been married for ten years and had two daughters and a son from that relationship. He had been divorced from his former wife, Maria, for six years. His few interests were reading, going to the movies, and spending most of his time with Jan.

John's parents immigrated to the United States in 1957 from Singapore, where they owned a small air-conditioning business. They opened a similar business in Hacienda Heights, near Los Angeles, where they resided. John has a younger sister, who he claimed lives in Germany to be away from the control of their parents. He also had a younger brother who killed himself. John blamed his parents for the suicide, saying that his brother could not live up to his parents' expectations.

In this segment of the interview I tried to join and help John relax by continuing to make supportive and sympathetic statements. It was evident from the discussion that his parents were traditional. They spoke Chinese at home, celebrated Chinese holidays, and socialized with Chinese friends. Based on this observation, I tried joining and conveying understanding by disclosing that my parents were immigrants and, like him, I was a first-generation Chinese American. I also said that my parents were very traditional, which was evidenced by their inability to accept my sister's marriage to a Caucasian.

In the problem stage of the interview, John described his treatment by his former therapist for chronic depression and preoccupation with suicidal thoughts. He said that antidepressants did not help and that both he and Mr. Kahle attributed his problems to John's inability to overcome the lack of validation and rejection he had felt from his parents throughout most of his life. For John, his parents' refusal to continue in family therapy was another indication of their lack of care and concern.

John described his parents as being critical, unsupportive, and unloving. He felt that he was always made to feel ashamed for not being able to meet their expectations and that he was never good enough. According to John, his parents didn't like his friends; his career choice; his former wife, Maria, who was Hispanic; or his current Caucasian partner, Jan. They refused to continue giving him financial support and were angry, believing that he was irresponsible and that the cure for his depression was to return to work and stop feeling sorry for himself.

During this stage of the interview, I tried using the solution-focused exception question in an attempt to change direction and discuss something positive. I told John that there must have been some exceptions to the way he described his father's treatment of him and asked him to describe times when he felt supported and felt his father's pride. He mentioned a few incidents, one of which happened when he won an outstanding academic achievement award in junior high school. However, he refused to say much when I asked him to expound how it felt to receive the award and know that his father was feeling proud. He indicated that the positive times were few and far between and therefore didn't add up to much. This showed me that he was unwilling or unable at this point to see anything positive regarding his parents. I tried to end this discussion on a positive note by saying that at least his father knows how to convey support and pride.

I asked John how he thought I could be of help, and he said that he hoped I could use my knowledge regarding Chinese families to get his parents to recognize their contribution to his problems and provide him with the support to resolve them. He further indicated that if I wasn't successful, he would have no choice but to kill himself. His response told me that he continued to remain angry toward his parents, accepted no responsibility for his behavior, and was helpless and dependent upon his parents to resolve his problems. As long as he remained in this position, he was powerless to do anything to change his feelings or his relationship with his parents.

I then shared my clinical observations with John and recommended a treatment plan. My major objective in this segment was to assist John in making major perceptual shifts and, in doing so, to have him perceive the problems and the solutions to them differently. I began by indicating to John that I didn't see his problem as chronic depression, but as chronic sadness. I went on to explain the difference between depression and sadness, the latter being associated with the loss of something we love or care about and the feelings of helplessness and loneliness associated with that loss. I believed that he felt the loss of love and support from his parents and was longing for it. He agreed.

This intervention organized John's problem into a workable solution. Instead of the problem being his parents' unwillingness to help him cure his depression, over which he had no control, it became his longing for unfulfilled love from his parents, a problem I could help him resolve with or without his parents' support.

I spent the major portion of the remainder of the session attempting to help John make a contextual shift; I described the differences between Chinese and Western culture and explained my belief that his problems were associated with his inability to integrate the two. I went on to say that from what he had described, his parents' child-rearing practices and the ways in which they related to him appeared to be based on Chinese values, norms, and beliefs. I told him that Chinese culture is shame-based, expects children to be compliant, has high performance expectations, and teaches that children should marry within their own ethnicity. I further explained that traditional Chinese parents do not share loving feelings or validate their children through verbal expression; they demonstrate care and concern by providing a safe and comfortable home environment and the means for their children to become successful.

I told John that Chinese parents generally believe that their children are always capable of improving on their performance and therefore tend to encourage improvement by criticism rather than praise. They also believe that talking about problems and trying to understand them are a waste of time and that the solution lies in taking action and doing something about them. Consequently, I told John, it did not surprise me to hear that his parents used shame as a controlling mechanism, were angry when he didn't choose the field they wanted him to enter and when he married Maria, and were critical even when he performed well. I also told him that it did not surprise me that his parents did not share their feelings in the family therapy session but instead indicated that they had provided a good home for him. Finally, I told him that his parents were not unusual and that most Chinese parents would expect him to return to work to cure his depression. I made it clear, however, that my impressions were based only on what he had described and that until I met his parents, I could not be sure of my diagnosis.

Throughout this segment, I tried to soften John's angry feelings toward his parents by saying that they may not have intended to be hurtful or unsupportive but instead were being guided by their cultural beliefs. I also tried to enhance his self-perception by normalizing his feelings.

I explained to John that whether or not my observations regarding his parents were true, I believed that he had internalized pathological shame. I then described what this meant and said that it was manifested in him in the following ways: (1) his need for validation and approval from his parents to feel good, (2) his need for them to admit that they were wrong rather than being able to stand on his own convictions regarding his perceptions, (3) his feelings of worthlessness, and (4) his wish to kill himself or cease to exist if he didn't receive acknowledgment from his parents. After much discussion, John agreed with my observations.

Following my clinical assessment, I told John that the goal of treatment would not be individuation but family integration, and that meant finding peace with his parents, regardless of whether or not they demonstrated the love he had yearned for throughout his life. I elaborated on the concept of family integration and on ways in which it could be achieved. Throughout the interview, John kept alluding to his belief that his parents didn't love him; therefore, he needed to decide whether or not his belief was true. I explained that there was a difference between believing and knowing something: the former is subject to change given certain evidence and the latter is fact.

If it was a fact that his parents didn't love him, it served no purpose to try to obtain from them what they could not give. Consequently, the goal of treatment would be to help him in grieving for what he would never receive from them, thereby helping him to find peace and integration. If he was in doubt, he would need to establish criteria based on Chinese rather than Western culture in order to determine whether or not his parents loved him. We then would examine their relationship based on those criteria so that a decision could be made. This may or may not have required a family therapy session with them. Finally, if he believed his parents loved him, the logical conclusion was that he was lovable and worthy. This also meant that he could now approach his parents in an inviting, peaceful, and accepting manner, maximizing opportunities for them to be supportive and understanding.

I explained to John that no matter what his decision was regarding his parents' feelings, he needed to approach them from a position of strength rather than weakness if he hoped to achieve family integration and peace within himself. The responsibility for resolving his problems would be dependent on him rather than his parents. Doing this required him to overcome his pathological shame, emotional turmoil, and psychological dependency upon his parents. These thus became the treatment goals.

John accepted my clinical observations and suggested treatment goals. He could not, however, decide whether or not his parents loved him. To help him come to a decision, I gave him the homework assignment of spending a half-hour alone each day reviewing and reflecting on his relationship with his parents throughout the years, followed by writing his thoughts and feelings in a journal. We would review his journal at the beginning of our next session.

In addition to assisting John in clarifying the issues with his parents, this exercise was designed to help him "be with" his feelings rather than merely reacting to them. This would make him feel less helpless and overwhelmed. We closed the session by agreeing to meet two hours each week because of the distance he had to travel to see me.

Subsequent Sessions

During the next three sessions, John could not decide whether or not his parents loved him. From what I read in his journal and observed in the sessions, it was obvious that he was in tremendous emotional pain. I provided a safe atmosphere in which he could express his deep feelings of sadness, despair, helplessness, and anger. I empathized and worked affectively with his emotions, using visual imagery and role playing to help him to verbalize and understand them. In the process, I was creating a corrective experience where he shared his insecure feelings of shame and abandonment and yet felt cared for and understood. I took on the role of being the father he had envisioned. I was also helping him to grieve and thereby to find peace with the painful experiences of his life.

Before proceeding with affective interventions, I explained to John the psychology underpinning emotions and how it would be useful for achieving our treatment objectives. In addition to working with him to address his emotional pain, I also developed a theme of pride to counter his feelings of shame. Combining cognitive restructuring and affective interventions, I continued to highlight and emphasize his accomplishments, positive attributes, and loving relationships. One homework assignment he completed was to list three dozen successes in the preceding five years. I also brought in Jan to describe his strengths and achievements and the reasons she loved him.

By the fifth session, John's emotional turmoil had significantly diminished, with his feelings no longer overriding his thought processes. He felt less shame and resentment in regard to his parents and concluded that he didn't know whether or not they loved him. We agreed that a family therapy session was needed to help him in making his decision. However, before that session, we worked on some of the criteria upon which he would make his determination. In our discussions, I described the importance of Confucian ethical principles and the Chinese cultural standards for success and achieving harmony. We also discussed and agreed on how he would engage his parents in a receptive manner. In the session, John would not be critical or ask for anything. Instead, the goal of the session would be to help him understand his parents' hopes and expectations regarding his future, their perceptions about their relationship with him, and their attempts to provide him with support.

It took three additional sessions to prepare John to meet his parents and to reduce his remaining fears and feelings of anger toward them. However, in the meantime, his parents refused to return to treatment.

John said that his parents liked the outdoors; therefore, I decided to send them a letter inviting them to lunch at my training center in Lake Arrowhead, located sixty-five miles east of Hacienda Heights. In the letter I said that I needed their assistance in helping to understand their son's problems. I thought they might accept my invitation because of the informal arrangement for the meeting and the fact that I was a professor and an expert in Chinese culture. However, when I called, they politely refused, saying that Mrs. Woo wasn't feeling well.

John was very close to and received support from his Uncle Fred, Mr. Woo's older brother. We were successful in using him as a go-between. With John's permission, I called his uncle, explaining to him John's problem and our inability to meet with his parents. I then asked for his assistance in arranging a meeting between him, me, John, and John's parents. I explained to him the purpose of the meeting and said that I would be very careful not to offend or bring shame upon his brother and sister-in-law. He agreed to help, and shortly thereafter he arranged for a meeting at his home on a Saturday when I had planned to be in the Hacienda Heights area to visit my family.

When I met John's parents, I told them that I was indebted to them for agreeing to the meeting and added that I knew it represented a deep concern for John's well-being. After joining and socializing, I explained the purpose of the meeting and then proceeded to John, who asked the series of questions we had prepared. The following questions were included in the list:

1. What did they see as John's strengths?
2. What did they see as his weaknesses?
3. How did they perceive his growing up?
4. When were they most proud of him?

5. When were they least proud of him?

6. How have they helped him through the years?

7. What did they attribute his current problems to?

8. How did they think he could overcome them?

9. What did they hope for him in the future?

Throughout the interview John politely asked exploratory questions while I highlighted the things that had been said that were positive and demonstrated care or concern on their part. The content of the discussion wasn't nearly as important as the fact that John was talking with his parents in a secure, respectful, and responsible manner, demonstrating psychological security and a high level of personal integration.

Toward the end of the session, John's parents were invited to ask questions. They politely refused, adding that they hoped the information they gave would be useful in helping their son. I closed by telling them to give me a call if they had any questions in the future.

In our next session, John told me that he didn't agree with everything his parents had said in the previous meeting but realized they had done the best they could. He also said that he didn't feel close to them and probably never would. However, he was going to maintain contact and be respectful. By his statements and demeanor, it was evident that he had achieved as much family integration as was possible by accurately assessing the nature of his relationship with his parents and the differences in their cultural contexts.

Throughout the remainder of the session and in the closing session the following week, we continued to explore the differences between Chinese and American culture and how he could integrate them. We also discussed what he had learned in treatment about himself and his relationship with his parents. Finally, we discussed what job opportunities were available to him, as he was ready to return to work.

This case describes the struggle of John Woo, who suffered for years from depression and emotional turmoil because of his inability to win approval from or reconcile his differences with his parents. He blamed them for his problems and perceived them as being rejecting, indifferent, and unsupportive. During the course of treatment, John learned to recognize his unrealistic expectations of his parents and to see that the problems between them were culturally related. His expectations of family support and interaction were based on a Western perspective, whereas theirs were based on a Chinese perspective. With this new information and other insights, John was able to find peace and achieve family integration by grieving over the loss of the loving relationship he desired with his parents; accepting the fact that he, and not his parents, was in charge of resolving his problems; and recognizing and appreciating the care and support his parents had demonstrated through the years. Although John had hoped to feel closer to his parents, he accepted what the relationship could offer, treated them with kindness and respect, and moved on with his life.

Chapter Eight

Divided Loyalty

A Couple in Crisis

This chapter tells the story of Robert Wang, age thirty-two, and Jill Wang, age twenty-nine, married for five years and with two children. The couple came to see me for marital therapy shortly after Jill's third hospitalization for what she called a mental breakdown. Like many Chinese Americans, this couple's problems were compounded by their having been caught in the middle of the different rules and expectations governing Western and Chinese marriages. This case illustrates the use of communication and problem-solving skills in helping such couples resolve differences and achieve family integration.

Western marriages are based on love, and roles are not clearly defined. The marital dyad is seen as an entity in itself, and couples often find themselves distanced from their families of origin. Couples move into a community, but most of their social, psychological, and recreational needs are met elsewhere. In addition, Western marriages have expectations of equality and thus require tremendous flexibility. It is common for couples to have major differences in many aspects of their life. Those differences as well as conflicts are resolved either by negotiation or by one partner making a loving sacrifice and putting her or his partner's needs first. Finally, emphasis is not on the "I" but rather the "we," with each partner striving to have his or her personal needs met in the relationship while growing in love.

Traditional Chinese marriages are based on functions, and roles are clearly defined. Such marriages are arranged for the benefit of the extended family. A person does not marry an individual but instead marries into a family that is an integral part of the community. It is not uncommon to have multiple generations living under one roof. Differences or conflicts are resolved arbitrarily by the head of the household, normally the father or a grandparent. Finally, satisfaction is achieved in traditional Chinese marriages when the expectations for marital roles are respected and fulfilled.

Initial Interview

The Wangs began treatment in a state of crisis, with Jill threatening to leave the relationship unless her requests were met. She was very angry and agitated, while Robert remained calm and somewhat aloof. I spent the first several minutes helping Jill to relax while obtaining background information. They had been close high school friends in Hong Kong but didn't fall in love until they immigrated and met here in the United States. They were married after a two-year courtship and the wedding was held in Hong Kong. However, Robert's mother disapproved of Jill, creating a strained relationship between them. Robert's defiance of his mother's wishes was a break in tradition and a movement toward modern thinking. Jill was in a program to obtain a master's degree in accounting; Robert owned and operated a foreign-automobile catalog business in Los Angeles, where they lived.

They had experienced minor marital problems since the inception of their marriage. Unfortunately, things became much worse two years later when, as a result of Robert's insistence, they allowed his nineteen-year-old niece from Hong Kong to come and live with them. It is customary among Chinese to allow relatives to move in when they are in need of assistance. Allowing his niece to live with them reflected Robert's traditional thinking. Mary, his niece, was to stay with them temporarily, after which she was to live permanently with another aunt. However, she was forced to remain with them when the aunt returned to Hong Kong. Arguments began to erupt when Jill complained to Robert about Mary's lack of cooperation, selfishness, and disrespectful behavior.

After several months of trying unsuccessfully to obtain her co-operation, Jill asked if Mary could be sent back to Hong Kong. Robert, who didn't believe her complaints about Mary, said that he was the head of the household and it was his decision that she re-main. Jill thought she had no alternative but to acquiesce to his rul-ing. Matters continued to worsen, with Jill believing that Robert was insensitive to her thoughts and feelings and more loyal to Mary and his mother. She also felt that he tried to avoid her angry out-bursts by working late. Problems reached a critical point when Jill was hospitalized for depression and suicidal ideations. This reflected the response of a Chinese woman who needed support and under-standing but who had no influence over a rigid and indifferent hus-band. It was her only means of being heard and supported. Shortly afterward, Robert's views changed when Mary was arrested with her friends for possession of narcotics.

Mary was sent home to Hong Kong; however, Robert's mother blamed Jill for the problems. Jill became enraged when she heard that she was being blamed and insisted that Robert defend her. He refused to so do.

When I asked them what they perceived to be the current prob-lems in the marriage, Jill said that she wanted Robert to help her overcome the resentful feelings she was still experiencing toward him for the nearly two years she spent not being understood or sup-ported. She also wanted Robert to defend her against his mother and to reestablish trust, which she believed was totally lacking in their relationship. Finally, she wanted to establish more mutual in-terests between them and wanted him to be more supportive, at-tentive, and affectionate.

On the basis of support and insights she had received from women friends and therapists in the hospital, Jill was determined to leave the relationship if her requests weren't met. Chinese women in this country quickly learn that Western culture does not support the subordination of women in relationships and that divorce is a realistic option for them. This awareness, coupled with their ability to support themselves financially, is fostering an increase in divorce among Chinese American couples.

Robert said that Jill was being unreasonable. He felt that his apology for not believing her when she complained about Mary should absolve him from her anger. He believed that if she stopped thinking about the bad times, things would get better. He also said that it would not be customary for him to defend Jill against his mother. This was an example of cultural camouflage. Robert had been willing to break with tradition to marry Jill against his mother's wishes because it served his aim; however, he now hid behind tradition as an excuse for not challenging his mother and defending Jill. He also felt that he had little time for developing more mutual interests with Jill because of the long hours he had to devote to the business. Finally, he believed that he was demonstrating care and concern for Jill by supporting her education and providing her with a comfortable lifestyle.

Robert's response to Jill's request was based on traditional Chinese beliefs: bad feelings are resolved by not dwelling on them and instead focusing on the positive; the role of a husband is that of a provider, and therefore his time should be devoted to earning a living rather than developing mutual interests with his wife. The husband does not demonstrate love or care by attentiveness or affection, but by providing his family with a comfortable home in which their practical needs are met.

I shared with the couple my belief that Jill had made a contextual shift in her beliefs and that now, as a result, each of them held a different view of the nature of the relationship, the role expectations for the spouses, and the way marital conflicts should be resolved. I explained that in the beginning of their marriage the relationship had appeared to be based on Chinese beliefs because it was hierarchical and their roles were clearly defined. However, as a result of her problems with Mary and her conversations with friends and therapists, Jill had changed and now wanted a more

Western marriage, based on equality, affection, and negotiation of differences.

The couple agreed with my observations and Robert indicated that he would be willing to make an effort to change and compromise. I tried unsuccessfully to make an affectionate bridge between them by asking them to describe the positive attributes that attracted them to one another. However, as they did this, Jill's resentment continued to manifest itself through angry outbursts and accusatory statements. I explained to the couple the way resentful and enraged feelings block the ability to communicate effectively and suggested that the first goal of treatment should be to help Jill to relinquish them. They agreed to this goal, along with the second goal of resolving their differences.

I used a desensitization program to help Jill with her negative feelings. I explained to the couple how the program worked and listed for them the following assumptions regarding feelings:

1. Feelings can be normal, abnormal or dysfunctional.
2. Individuals can experience single or multiple feelings.
3. Individuals can experience mixed or confused feelings.
4. Feelings can be misleading or can help individuals to discover deeper truths.
5. Feelings can be expressed through our body and can create physical pain or damage.
6. Feelings can be layered.
7. Feelings can influence how we behave.
8. Feelings can be complementary.
9. All feelings are reasonable and meaningful.
10. Feelings can allow for the negotiation of differences.

Jill was to set aside a half-hour each day to do the assigned work. First, she was to list everything about which she felt resentful. This helped her to compartmentalize the issues and made them feel less overwhelming. Second, she was to take each issue and spend fifteen minutes concentrating on it, allowing herself to experience the feelings associated with her thoughts. Third, she was to externalize her feelings by both writing them in a journal and verbalizing them to herself. Fourth, she was to share her experience with Robert when he returned home from work. He was instructed to simply listen and not try to fix her pain. She was to continue in this manner until she no longer felt enraged at the particular issues on which she was focused. Finally, she was to bring the list to the next session.

Subsequent Sessions

In the following session, Jill reported that she had only done the assignment three times and was still feeling very resentful. Robert added that it was very difficult for him to simply listen to her anger. I then provided individuation therapy, working directly with Jill to explore and externalize her resentful feelings. This modeled for Robert how to use reflective listening skills. This and the following sessions were devoted to this process. Jill was also encouraged to continue the work at home and, in an effort to reconnect the couple in a positive manner, Robert was asked to take his family on a weekend outing. Chinese typically include children in recreational activities. My assignment respected the manner in which the couple related. Jill and Robert enjoyed their children, and raising them was one area in which they worked cooperatively.

By the fourth session, Jill's resentful feelings had dissipated. We then turned our attention to our second goal, resolving the couple's differences. To achieve this goal, I used behavioral therapy to teach them communication and problem-solving skills. They were each to develop a list of problems they wished to address and then combine the list, ranking the problems from the most to the least serious. In the following session we would begin to address each issue, working from the least to the most serious. In most instances, it is not the issues themselves that create the problems between couples, but their inability to effectively communicate and problem-solve those issues. Three times during the week, Robert and Jill were to set aside one hour for practicing the skills they had learned in treatment. The sessions were to be audiotaped and reviewed by the couple during the week. Taping the interviews helped the couple to recall the sessions, particularly the instructions I had given them about communicating effectively. I closed the session by discussing problems associated with poor communication. This included issues related to asking rhetorical questions, operating from negative or closed mindsets, and sharing versus telling their partner about their feelings.

The fifth through ninth sessions were devoted to resolving the issues on the couple's problem sheet. To begin, they were given the following list of poor and positive communication patterns to study:

Poor Patterns

1. Involving others in the discussion
2. Interrupting your partner's discussion
3. Cross-complaining
4. Bringing up the past
5. Mind-reading
6. Lecturing
7. Using derogatory names
8. Making threats
9. Detouring from the issue being discussed
10. Attempting to make your partner feel ashamed

Positive Patterns

1. Being accepting
2. Giving praise
3. Being willing to listen
4. Clearly stating likes and dislikes
5. Acknowledging mistakes
6. Paraphrasing

7. Disengaging from no-win discussions

8. Talking with your partner

9. Being respectful of your partner's thoughts though you may disagree with them

10. Making "I" statements

These lists were used to point out to Robert and Jill how they communicated. In the following excerpt from an interview with Jill and Robert, the couple focused on Jill's desire for more support from Robert in raising their children:

Jill: I always have to beg you to help me with the kids. Can't you see how tired I am and just help?

Robert: [*He rolls his eyes and sighs in frustration.*] Well, I'm tired too. Can't you understand how tired I am when I come home? Besides, it's been very busy lately and I have so much to do.

Jill: You're always busy. It's just an excuse.

Marshall: Hold it. I can see already that this discussion isn't going anywhere. First, Jill, you didn't state clearly what you wanted. Instead you complained about not getting any help. This was followed by a rhetorical question. That put Robert on the defensive. By the way, I'm not faulting you. What I'm saying about good and poor communication skills is for both of you.

I can tell by your nonverbal messages, Robert, that you believed you were being attacked. [*I purposefully said "you believed" rather than "you felt" because Robert is "left-brained" and relates cognitively.*] You rolled your eyes and gave a sigh of frustration. You then countercomplained and, like Jill, followed with a rhetorical question. Next, you detoured from the subject by telling Jill how busy you were.

You, Jill, then went for the detour and complained that Robert was always busy. I bet you both felt [*for Jill*] or thought [*for Robert*] you weren't being heard.

Jill: That's true.

Marshall: You can get into trouble so quickly. Be sure to listen to
the tape. I'm listing things for you to remember. You can also
refer to the list I gave you. Remember, don't complain but
state your needs clearly and succinctly. No rhetorical questions, detouring, or cross-complaints. Robert, am I making
sense? [*This is an effort to punctuate my observations.*]

Robert: Yes.

Marshall: Do either of you have any questions?

Jill: No.

Robert: Uh, no, it makes sense.

Marshall: Okay, let's start over. Jill, state your needs. By the way,
Robert, the next issue we will address will be yours. [*This is to
maintain balance in the session.*]

Jill: I want more help with the kids. I feel all I'm doing is studying
and taking care of them. I want some time to go to the gym
and relax.

Robert: Well, why don't you cut back on your classes?

Jill: I can't if I want to graduate by next year. Besides, it's easier
for you to make time.

Marshall: Hold it again. Let me ask you, Jill, do you believe
Robert heard you?

Jill: No.

Marshall: Why?

Jill: Well, I'm not sure. I just feel he didn't.

Marshall: Well, he actually did. He suggested a solution that implied that he heard your problem. There are two problems
with this. First, his acknowledgment was indirect rather than
direct. If you two trusted one another it would probably
work. But because you don't, it must be made explicit. So,
Robert, the response should have been something like this:
"I hear what you said and I know you need some time to
relax." Second, offering a solution is premature at this time.
You're not into the brainstorming phase of the discussion
yet. That phase begins when you both have a clear understanding of the problem and are ready to look at alternatives.

At that point, you both list as many alternatives as you can without eliminating any. Then you proceed to go over the list, discussing the merit of each suggestion. If it's a long list, you cut it down to a short one and begin the process again. Then you agree on a final solution.

It's crazy sometimes. Robert, your intentions were good when you offered a solution, but Jill walked away from the exchange not feeling understood. [*Again I use the term* feeling *to identify with Jill.*] I know I'm saying a lot. Am I making any sense to you?

Robert: Yes.

Marshall: I'm glad it's on tape. Let's try once more.

I continued to work with Robert and Jill in this manner until they found a solution. Robert agreed to leave work on time on Tuesdays and Thursdays and, after having relaxed a few minutes, to assist in taking care of the children. They also agreed to extend child care two extra hours on the days Jill went to school.

By the time treatment ended, Jill and Robert hadn't resolved all their issues, but they believed they had learned the skills they needed to do so. Feeling supported, Jill no longer demanded that Robert support her against his mother. In turn, Robert tried to make himself more available to Jill and the children. In light of the understanding and support they were demonstrating to one another, it was evident that they were well on their way to achieving family integration. In the closing session, I reiterated the difficulty of finding peace in a marriage and integrating Chinese and Western cultural beliefs.

Chapter Nine

An Infant's Cry

A Case of Child Abuse

This chapter tells the story of the Chow family, who came to the attention of the authorities when eleven-month-old Katherine was seen in the emergency room for fractured legs. Her parents, Greg Chow, age thirty-six, and Dorothy Chow, age thirty-one, claimed she had rolled off their bed. However, medical evidence indicated that Katherine could only have sustained such an injury by having her limbs pulled and twisted. Mr. Chow was arrested and the family was reported to child protective services. Katherine and the couple's two other children, Christopher, age twelve, and Staci, age ten, were removed from their home and placed in protective custody with Mr. Chow's parents, Jock and Shirley. As shameful as it was for the grandparents, it was they who had initially reported the abuse and insisted that the child be brought to medical care.

This case illustrates Mrs. Chow's success in making a contextual shift in which she recognized that she could not achieve family integration with an abusive and indifferent husband. She was able to assess her cultural context and learn to integrate Western ideas into her Chinese upbringing. In so doing, she was able to achieve family integration and establish a safe and harmonious home for herself and her children.

In his initial interrogation, Mr. Chow admitted the allegation. His parents had suspected the abuse. After they confronted him with it, he angrily told them to leave his apartment. Frightened of their son's behavior, they complied. In the jurisdictional hearing that followed Mr. Chow's arrest, Mrs. Chow was found guilty of endangering Katherine for failing to report the abuse to the authorities.

She told the juvenile court that she had been afraid to do so for fear of being abused herself. The court took legal custody of the children while placing Katherine in the physical custody of her paternal grandparents. Staci and Christopher were returned home on the condition that Mrs. Chow attend parent education classes and participate in personal therapy for herself and family therapy for herself and the children.

Mr. Chow was released on bail and shortly afterward reversed his story and obtained a lawyer to defend him in criminal court. In the meantime, his parents and his wife stood behind him and reversed their stories as well. This is a common phenomenon. The nonabusing family members want the abuse to stop and initially welcome the referral to social services. They do not realize that social services is mandated to cross-report to law enforcement. However, once the child has been protected, they do not wish the perpetrator to be held accountable, or to be involved themselves in a criminal hearing.

The juvenile court prohibited Mr. Chow from seeing Katherine unsupervised. Furthermore, if he wished Katherine to be returned home, he would need to attend an extensive anger management program, accompany his wife to parent education classes, and participate in family therapy. He initially agreed to the conditions of the court.

Initial Interview

The initial interview was attended by Mrs. Chow and her two children, Christopher and Staci. Mrs. Chow conveyed that her husband could not attend because of a meeting with his lawyer. I took this as a sign of his resistance to participating in treatment. I joined and socialized with the family while gathering background information. Mrs. Chow reported that she was raised in Guangdong, China, before immigrating to Hong Kong with her mother at the age of seventeen. After working for a year in a sewing factory, she was "introduced" to Mr. Chow, who had been sent to Hong Kong by his parents to marry. Mr. Chow had been born in Hong Kong but had lived in the United States since the age of six. The Chows were married, and shortly afterward they returned to the United States. Initially, they lived with his parents, but after the birth of Christopher, they moved into their own apartment. Mrs. Chow was primarily a homemaker, though at times she worked in a sewing factory to supplement the family's income. She had no friends and spent her leisure time socializing with her in-laws and watching Chinese television programs.

Christopher and Staci were quiet, shy, respectful, and compliant. Court reports indicated that Christopher's school had filed a report with child protective services stating the school's belief that he had been abused. However, there was insufficient evidence to take any action. In the interview, Staci sat very close to her mother, often reaching over to hold her hand, while Christopher looked at his mother before answering any questions. It was evident that a nurturing relationship existed between the children and their mother. Even with their mother's encouragement, it took several minutes to draw them out and make them comfortable. They reported doing well in school but having few friends and interests. Like their mother, they spent most of their leisure time watching television and socializing with their extended family.

I respected the intergenerational and marital boundaries in the family by asking the children to leave before I talked with Mrs. Chow about their father. I asked her about her relationship with her husband and the allegations made in the court's report. She stood by her story that he hadn't abused Katherine. However, she did say that he had a bad temper and that the children were frightened of him. She also said that he was abusive to her, they shared no common interests, and she took the major responsibility for rearing the children. Later I learned that he took her earnings and gambled with them. Her responses to any questions regarding Mr. Chow were short and to the point. It was clear that she was uncomfortable talking about him, so I changed directions and asked her questions about the children. In discussing them, she became more animated and more elaborate in her responses. It was evident that she loved and took pride in them.

When I asked her why she was in treatment and how I could be of service to her, Mrs. Chow said that the family was ordered to attend as a condition of having Katherine returned home. Mrs. Chow didn't have any goals in mind for treatment, stating that her husband had all the ideas. Suspecting that Mr. Chow made the decisions in the family, I told her that we would wait for his input.

My diagnostic impression was that Mrs. Chow was a warm, nurturing, intelligent, and perceptive woman. Structurally, there was rigid boundary keeping between Mr. Chow and the rest of the family. He was seldom at home, and when he was, everyone worked to avoid his presence. The relationship between the couple appeared exploitative, with Mr. Chow using his wife to meet his selfish needs. She was in a traditional Chinese marriage and felt powerless and inferior. To counter her feelings of inferiority, I spent the remainder of the session having Mrs. Chow share her life story with me. The aim of this intervention was to get her to draw attention to herself and to begin to recognize her importance, strengths, and positive attributes. As she shared her story, I highlighted her talents, abilities, and personal qualities. I also began to develop the theme of competency to help in empowering her, pointing out everything that indicated her competency.

Subsequent Sessions

Mr. Chow appeared in the second session with his wife and two older children. The family's fear of him was evident. He dominated the discussion while Mrs. Chow and the children sat rigidly and quietly. I tried joining him by acknowledging how difficult it had to be for him to attend treatment. However, he immediately began to express anger about what he called false accusations and about everything he was being required to do by the juvenile court. He blamed his parents for these problems because they had reported him to child protective services. If they hadn't, he would not be facing criminal charges. Furthermore, he believed that the police were conspiring against him, trying to find someone to blame for his daughter's fractures.

I tried again to join with him while gathering background information. He would only state that he had difficulty holding a job as a mechanic because his superiors either were prejudiced, blamed him for problems he did not create, or found reasons not to like him. He wanted to know how counseling was going to help get his daughter back. I shared the reasons why families normally seek treatment. He said that he didn't have any problems or issues to examine, knew how to parent, and had a good relationship with his wife and children. I explained to him that therapy was only useful to those who wanted assistance in resolving personal or family problems. He reiterated that he had none and that all he wanted was to return home and be left alone.

I then said that I couldn't be of service to him and that unless he had personal or family problems that needed to be addressed, I wouldn't continue with him in treatment. He immediately replied that if treatment stopped, he wouldn't be able to return home or get custody of his daughter. I told him that I was sorry, but it was not my problem. I asked him to think about what I had said and told him that I wanted to see his parents at our next meeting to find out how Katherine was adjusting to the separation. I also wanted to see Katherine to assess her relationship with him and Mrs. Chow. Before ending the first thirty minutes of the session, I briefly chatted with Mrs. Chow, asking her to remember our discussion the previous week. Therapists using CAFT end when the work is completed, which in many instances is well before the scheduled fifty to sixty minutes have been reached. Asking Mrs. Chow to remember our previous week's discussion was an attempt to remind her of her strengths.

My clinical impressions of Mr. Chow were that he was insensitive, rigid, unperceptive, irresponsible, and hostile. It was evident that he took no responsibility for his behavior and didn't have any desire to be in treatment. Telling Mr. Chow that I couldn't be of service to him was a strategic intervention using the technique of logical conclusion. I wasn't going to debate with Mr. Chow or try to convince him that he needed treatment. My instinct and clinical observations told me that this would be useless, putting the responsibility for defining the family's problems and the goals for treatment on me instead of on him, where it belonged. By refusing to treat Mr. Chow or take responsibility for his dilemma, I was forcing him to either define some treatment goals or accept the consequences of not being treated. It also sent the clear message that I was going to maintain my neutrality and not side with him or those with whom he was angry. Asking him to return the following week with Katherine and his parents gave him time to decide in which direction he wished to go.

The entire family attended the third session. It was evident immediately that Mrs. Chow and Katherine had a warm and nurturing relationship. After briefly socializing with everyone, I asked Christopher and Staci to wait in the reception area. I then explained to the grandparents why I had asked them to attend the session and told them that I wanted any information that would be useful to me in helping the family to be reunited and achieve integration. Mr. Chow's father immediately began explaining the difficulties they had with their son throughout the years. He described his son as being irresponsible, unable to hold a job, and disrespectful as well as being a womanizer, a gambler, and a heavy drinker. Before I could intervene and change the focus, Mr. Chow became infuriated and walked out of the session. His father said that this outburst was an example of his son's temper. He had pushed his son to marry, hoping he would become responsible by taking on the duties of a husband and father. Now he hoped that the programs his son was required to participate in would teach him responsibility and appropriate behavior. Mr. Chow's mother insisted that he was a good boy who only needed help. Both of them said that they had little influence over their son, adhering to their position of not believing that he was guilty of abusing Katherine. After gathering more background information from the grandparents and answering their questions regarding what their son could expect from the criminal and juvenile courts, I asked to speak with Mrs. Chow alone. I felt that at this point in the case, the grandparents would be of little assistance in treatment. Although it is not customary, I thought it was important to see Mrs. Chow alone, believing that she would feel very hesitant about speaking with Mr. Chow's parents in the room.

I asked Mrs. Chow what she was planning to do if her husband didn't participate in therapy; she said she didn't know. She did want Katherine back and would do anything required to have her returned. After highlighting the care and dedication she had toward her children, I told her I would ask Ms. Putman, the child protective services worker responsible for her case, to meet with us the following week to discuss the stipulations of the reunification plan. I also said that I hoped her husband would attend the session.

In the fourth session, Mrs. Chow said that her husband refused to return to treatment. Ms. Putman then outlined the stipulations in the reunification plan. Mrs. Chow was required to attend parent education classes to learn how to help and protect her children and how to encourage them to be more "spontaneous and independent." Family therapy was set up to help her and her husband develop a more supportive relationship by learning to communicate more effectively. Personal therapy was recommended for her to develop self-esteem and assertiveness skills so that the juvenile court could have some assurance that she would protect her children against the possible abuse of their father. However, now that her husband had refused to comply with the court's mandates, the only way Katherine would be returned home would be if Mrs. Chow and her husband separated.

Following Ms. Putman's departure, I explored Mrs. Chow's options with her, explaining that she was being asked to make a contextual shift and to make changes that were contrary to her cultural beliefs. Throughout the discussion I was careful not to tell her what to do; otherwise, I would be keeping her in a dependent and subordinate position. Instead, I used reflective listening skills to model what it was like to be in a relationship where her needs and desires were considered important. Furthermore, believing that the major motivation for her wanting to change would be her concern for the well-being of the children, I asked questions directed at helping her to decide what was best for them.

Mrs. Chow decided to continue in treatment even if her husband objected. This was significant because it indicated the beginning of a shift in cultural context, assertiveness, and a movement toward some independence. Fortunately, her husband did not object.

The next three sessions were spent helping Mrs. Chow to continue examining her options and to find the support she felt was necessary to achieve her objective of having Katherine returned home. We also had discussions on the differences between Chinese and Western culture and the advantages and disadvantages of both. In the sixth session, Mrs. Chow made a major contextual shift and decided as a treatment goal to achieve more independence from her husband and his parents. To help accomplish this goal, she decided to enroll in an English as a Second Language program to improve her English and, based on a suggestion from me, she joined a women's support group. I assisted her in locating a language class and support group near her home. She also began watching American rather than Chinese programs to improve her English. We agreed to meet every three weeks, with my major focus being to help her integrate and understand the changes taking place in her life. Throughout treatment I kept emphasizing her competency and ability to make appropriate decisions.

Two months later, Mrs. Chow asked my advice about whether or not she should divorce her husband. She was being encouraged to do so by the women in her support group. I told her that I wouldn't give an opinion but would help her examine the issues upon which she would make her decision. In this manner I kept fostering autonomy rather than dependency. She questioned getting a divorce because she feared Mr. Chow's and his parents' response, divorce's legal ramifications, its stigma, the impact it would have on the children, how she would support herself, and how she would live her life. I obtained free legal advice for her, and in the meantime, we spent the next three sessions examining the issues she had raised. However, she still remained undecided after these sessions. I told her that it was normal to be ambivalent because this was a life-changing decision. With things proceeding calmly in her life, we agreed to suspend therapy for three months. However, I told her that she could call and talk with me on the phone or return anytime she thought it was necessary.

Mrs. Chow returned ten weeks later; she wanted my help in divorcing her husband, who was now living with another woman. Mrs. Chow recognized and accepted that he would not change and said that she no longer wished to live under such exploitative conditions. She also recognized that the only way to have Katherine returned home was to end the marriage. She had hoped, with my assistance, to receive permission from the juvenile court to live with Mr. Chow's parents, assuming they would allow it, until she could support herself. Through the advice of one of the women in her support group, she was going to obtain a certificate in hairstyling and then seek employment as a hairstylist. We agreed that the best way to proceed was to first tell Mr. Chow's parents of her decision and then try to elicit their support. Through the use of role playing, I tried to prepare Mrs. Chow for the various responses we might anticipate from them.

In the session that followed, Mr. Chow's parents appeared to be disappointed but not surprised by her decision. As we had anticipated, they thought she should remain in the marriage because of the shame that would be brought on the family. Mrs. Chow supported their beliefs but adhered to her decision to proceed with the divorce. After much discussion, they supported her decision and agreed to let her live with them. Their decision was based in part on their concern for the well-being of their grandchildren, their belief that their son was not going to change, and their wish not to have the full responsibility for raising Katherine. Mrs. Chow's father-in-law agreed to tell his son about the divorce. When he was told, Mr. Chow said that he didn't care.

I sent a report to Ms. Putman, summarizing the changes that had taken place in the Chow family, and informed her of Mrs. Chow's decision to divorce her husband. I also outlined and supported Mrs. Chow's plans to reunite the family. Later, Mrs. Chow, the grandparents, and I met with Ms. Putman to discuss the report and the suggested reunification plan. She agreed with the plan and recommended to the court that Katherine be returned to the physical custody of her mother.

I spent the final three sessions providing divorce therapy for Mrs. Chow and her children. The children were both sad and relieved that their father was no longer going to live with them. Mrs. Chow held no animosity toward her soon-to-be ex-husband and was just relieved that the relationship had ended. His departure, coupled with what Mrs. Chow had learned from the parent education classes, already had a noticeable effect on them. They were more relaxed, spontaneous, and playful. It was obvious that Mrs. Chow and her children had finally achieved family integration. At his criminal court trial a year later, Mr. Chow was found guilty of abusing Katherine and was given two years' probation.

This case demonstrates how Mrs. Chow, a victim of domestic violence, was able to make a radical shift from a traditional to a more modern worldview in a short period of time. The emphasis in treatment was on empowering Mrs. Chow and helping her to assess the family and cultural context in which she lived. In her examination, she recognized the need to divorce Mr. Chow in order to protect herself and her children and achieve family integration. Case management interventions consisted of helping her to find the resources and skills she needed to live an independent life and using divorce therapy to help her and her children find peace with the breakup of the family.

Chapter Ten

Irreconcilable Differences

The Liu Family

This chapter tells the story of Edward Liu, a thirty-six-year-old man who was unable to reconcile the differences between his Chinese upbringing and his yearning for independence and personal happiness. His problem became a crisis after he learned that his second wife, Candice, had filed for divorce. This case illustrates the use of Chinese American Family Therapy in helping Ed to accept the loss of his second marriage and to bridge the differences between family and personal expectations.

Ed is the oldest of three children. His parents reside in San Francisco, while his brother David, a physician, lives in Riverside with his Japanese American wife, Naomi, and their two children. His sister Kristin, an attorney, lives in San Jose with her Chinese American husband and their one child. At the time of treatment, Ed was living temporarily with his brother and was in the process of moving his family from San Francisco to the Los Angeles area.

Ed was brought to see me by David and Naomi after he overdosed on sleeping pills. He had attempted suicide two days after receiving his divorce papers and four days before a scheduled visit from his mother. Fortunately, Ed shared his suicidal ideations with his brother shortly before his attempt. David called Ed at work to see how he was doing and discovered that he had taken the afternoon off. Suspicious, he rushed home to find Ed unconscious, with a suicide note apologizing for bringing pain and shame on his family. Paramedics were called in time to revive him. Ed was then taken to the Riverside General Hospital inpatient psychiatric ward for twenty-four-hour observation. He returned to work the next day to keep occupied and to prevent his mother and the rest of the family from knowing what had happened.

Initial Interview

Ed was brought to see me by David and Naomi three days after his suicide attempt. He was clearly depressed and feeling remorseful for having tried to kill himself. In the initial phase of the session, I used crisis intervention techniques to support him and normalize his thoughts and feelings. I also examined the extent to which he was still feeling suicidal. I then proceeded to obtain background information regarding his family life and marriages.

Ed immigrated with his parents from Hong Kong to San Francisco at the age of two. His parents opened and operated a small grocery store, which they still own. Ed and his siblings worked in the store from the time they were old enough until they went to college. Ed described his parents as having an extensive family and social network. Both he and his brother described them as being traditional, with very high expectations for them and their sister. They also described their father as being strict but unassuming, and their mother as domineering and controlling.

Ed recalled always having to put his family's needs before his own personal desires, even when he felt that his parents were being unreasonable. He could not participate in extracurricular activities in school because he had to work in the store. He wanted to major in graphic arts but was discouraged from doing so because his parents didn't consider it practical. He therefore majored in electrical engineering. He was the one his parents depended upon for any assistance. For example, he would be responsible for ensuring that the family had proper health insurance or for accompanying his mother to the doctors and learning about her medical problems from them. Ed's first attempt at some personal freedom was his decision to attend the University of California at Los Angeles (UCLA). Rather than having to confront his parents with his desire for more autonomy, he could use his enrollment at UCLA as a legitimate and practical reason for leaving home. However, upon graduation, he was pressured to return.

In college Ed dated non-Chinese women but was careful not to become seriously involved, knowing that his parents would disapprove of an interethnic marriage, as they later demonstrated with his brother's marriage to Naomi. Shortly after his return home, Ed learned that his mother had arranged for him to visit Hong Kong with her to meet a women he might select to marry. Initially he balked at the idea of an arranged marriage, but eventually he acquiesced to his parents' wishes. He and his wife Sandra lived with his parents until their divorce six years later.

According to Ed and David, Sandra was treated harshly and indifferently by their mother. In addition to working in the store, Sandra was responsible for cooking, fulfilling most of the other household responsibilities, and meeting the needs of their mother. Accustomed to accepting his parents' behavior and demands, Ed felt helpless to do anything about his wife's circumstances. Although he found Sandra kind and caring, he felt little attraction toward her. He also believed that they had little in common, particularly in light of the difference in their education: he had a master's degree and she had only a high school diploma. Consequently, both of them were unhappy in the relationship. Even the birth of their two children, Raymond and Alice, didn't bring them closer together. To help cope with the dissatisfaction in his life, Ed kept busy by working long hours.

Four years into the marriage, Ed and Sandra were devastated by the sudden loss of their two-year-old daughter, Alice, who died of heart disease. Following Alice's death, Mrs. Liu became harsher with Sandra, blaming her for bringing bad luck into the family. Two years later, no longer able to tolerate the abuse by her mother-in-law and her unhappiness in the marriage, Sandra asked for a divorce. She took Raymond and moved in with her parents and sister, who had immigrated to the United States and made their home in Oakland. Ed took responsibility for the failure of the marriage and felt ashamed about it; however, realizing how miserable Sandra had been in the relationship, he was pleased about her decision.

Shortly following their divorce, Ed initiated his second attempt at achieving some independence and personal happiness. Against his parents' wishes, he moved into his own apartment. However, like so many of his generation, he continued to be involved with his parents, visiting them frequently and responding to their every request.

Two years after his divorce, Ed thought he had finally found the happiness he was seeking. At a party, he met and fell in love with Candice. At the time, she was divorcing a husband who had been physically and emotionally abusive. Ed and Candice had a whirlwind relationship and were married immediately following her divorce. As expected, Ed's parents objected to the relationship because Candice was not only Caucasian but divorced, with a six-year-old child.

Ed and Candice's problems started early in their marriage. Candice found Ed's family to be intrusive and insensitive to her needs. She was especially resentful over the fact that at family gatherings Ed's son Raymond received a great deal of attention while her son Lawrence was ignored. She also resented what she considered to be Ed's excessive involvement with his parents.

Candice constantly raised issues of loyalty, making Ed feel he was in a no-win situation. By pleasing and remaining loyal to his family, he would alienate and have problems with Candice. However, if he acquiesced to his wife's demand that he put her needs before his family's, he would feel guilty and ashamed for abandoning his obligations and responsibilities. Trying to please both parties only created more problems and unhappiness in the relationship.

Problems worsened in the marriage after the birth of their son Roger. Candice believed that Mr. and Mrs. Liu used their desire to be with their new grandson as an excuse to control Ed's behavior even more and to intrude on their life. Ed's attempt to explain to his wife that his parents' behavior was normal in Chinese culture did nothing to rectify matters. Finally, Candice threatened to leave the relationship if her needs were not put first.

To accommodate his wife's demand, Ed decided to take a promotion in a company office in Los Angeles. The transfer provided him with a reasonable excuse for leaving the area where his parents lived and saved him from having to bring shame or pain to his parents. He planned to move to Los Angeles and live with his brother David until Candice could transfer or find a job and follow him. However, a month after moving to Los Angeles, he was served with divorce papers.

When asked what he wanted from treatment, Ed said that he needed assistance in finding a way to make Candice reconsider her decision. (This is a typical early response by a loving spouse who does not want a divorce.) He believed that without his marriage, life was meaningless. He saw himself as a failure, unable to please his parents; his first wife, Sandra; and now his second wife, Candice. He also felt guilty and ashamed of causing his children to be raised in a divorced family. He was feeling powerless and thought the only way he could avoid being a failure and bringing further shame on himself and his family was to make his second marriage successful.

My clinical impression was that Ed was an intelligent, sensitive, caring, and insightful individual. Through most of his life he was a traditionalist, a Chinese American who had strongly internalized Chinese values (Sue and Sue, 1973). His identity and self-worth were primarily associated with his family involvement. He worked at being the good son, always putting the needs of his family before his own. Even his obligations in his first marriage remained secondary to the demands and authority of his parents.

Like many other traditionalists, Ed's emotional problems arose out of the fact that he often acquiesced to his parents' wishes even when he believed they were unreasonable. Unable to challenge his parents for fear of feeling guilty or ashamed, he could not reconcile the differences between his own beliefs and desire for personal happiness and his parents' expectations. Consequently, he couldn't find peace and happiness by continuing to remain loyal to his family heritage. Instead, he felt burdened and emotionally imprisoned in his duties and responsibilities, even when he moved out of his parents' home following his first divorce.

Ed's marriage to Candice represented his third major attempt to escape from his emotional prison and find personal happiness.

However, he still couldn't divorce himself from the loyalty and responsibility he felt toward his family. Sadly, rather than providing fulfillment, the marriage only exacerbated his inability to integrate his Chinese and American worlds. Consequently, his pending divorce represented not only the end of a marriage, but his inability to live in either world. Like many traditionalists, Ed couldn't blame his parents for his problems and unhappiness. Having no world in which to find peace and satisfaction and having no one to blame but himself for the guilt and shame he experienced, Ed wanted to end his life.

My immediate concern was Ed's suicidal ideations. Although he was not lethal, I believed he was at a very high risk for killing himself. He agreed not to commit suicide and to allow David, Naomi, and me to monitor his behavior for two weeks. I told them about the stages of grief and what they could expect during the next two months. I also instructed David and Naomi on ways they could provide Ed with emotional support. I then focused on Ed's request and helped him to develop a plan of action that would maximize the opportunity for Candice to reconsider her decision.

Ed agreed to send Candice a brief letter indicating why he wanted the marriage to continue, saying what he would do to support her needs, and stating his desire to meet with her to discuss what he had written. The meeting place would be her choice. He would give her a week to think about his request before calling her.

Subsequent Sessions

Ed attended the second session, held two days later, alone. We reviewed the letter he was sending to Candice. It was well written, clearly defining the issues he wished to convey. He informed me that he hadn't told his mother of Candice's decision and wasn't going to until he was sure there was no possibility of a reconciliation. I then focused my attention on giving Ed reasons to live if Candice proceeded with the divorce. This was accomplished by asking him to describe his relationship with his children, what he hoped for them, and how he imagined they would feel having to tell everyone the rest of their life that their father had committed suicide. To create an affective tie, I had him show me a picture of the children and describe what they were like. Among other things, he said that he had a good relationship with them, including Lawrence, whom he perceived as being his child. He also said that he wouldn't want them to feel the shame or embarrassment of having to explain his death. After a long discussion, Ed concluded that he had a responsibility to live for his children and to try to ensure that they had a better future.

In the remainder of the session, I used cognitive-restructuring interventions in an attempt to change Ed's negative perceptions of himself. I emphasized his sense of responsibility, loyalty, and family-centeredness. To counter his thoughts about being a failure, I gave him the homework assignment of thinking about ten things he had accomplished in life. We concluded the session by agreeing to meet the day following his telephone call to Candice.

David and Naomi brought Ed to the third session because he wanted to discontinue therapy after having spoken with Candice. She had said that she no longer loved him and wanted to move on with her life. In addition to being overwhelmed by Candice's decision, Ed was also feeling ashamed and humiliated over the criticism he was receiving from his mother, who had learned from David about the divorce and the suicide attempt.

I continued to use supportive interventions to normalize and provide support for Ed's thoughts and feelings. He assured me that based on our last meeting, he wasn't going to commit suicide. However, he was feeling extremely depressed and didn't know what to do with his life. I said he was in no position to make any decisions now; he first needed to work through the painful feelings he was experiencing. I again explained to the three of them what Ed could expect to feel over the next six to eight weeks. Ed refused hospitalization; therefore, we devised a treatment plan to ensure his safety and to ensure that he received support until our next session.

Ed continued to see me both alone and with David and Naomi in subsequent sessions. However, he refused to invite his mother to treatment, believing that it would be humiliating for both of them. Part of each session focused on divorce therapy, helping him to pass through the stages of loss and grief and resolving the various concerns associated with a divorce. These included issues related to the impact of the divorce on his children, family, and friendships.

During the next few weeks, Ed continued to feel extremely depressed over the loss of Candice. One weekend he returned to San Francisco to see her, but she refused to meet with him. However, by our seventh session, he was beginning to feel better. I asked if there was anything else I could do besides continuing to provide him with supportive therapy and helping him through the divorce process. He said that he wanted help in deciding whether or not he should return to San Francisco, where his parents now wanted him to live. He also wanted help with the shame and guilt he was feeling because he had failed at his second marriage and because of the criticism he was receiving from his mother.

I shared with Ed my view that in addition to the divorce, the basis for his unhappiness was his inability to successfully integrate his traditional Chinese beliefs with his modern ones. This prevented him from finding peace in either the Chinese or Western worlds. I also said that if he learned to blend the two worlds, he would know where to live. After a lengthy discussion, he agreed with my observations and added a final treatment goal of integrating his Chinese and Western values. However, I believed that before he addressed this issue, Ed had to first overcome his feelings of failure and then master his feelings of shame and guilt. With this in mind, I closed the session by asking him to continue with the homework assignment I had given him previously. He was to list ten major accomplishments in his life, reflect on them, and bring the list to the following session.

During the first segment of the eighth session, we examined Ed's homework assignment. The exercise and our discussion helped him to recognize that he had failed at some things but was not a "failure." In the second half of the session, I used a number of cognitive-restructuring interventions to help Ed overcome his feelings of guilt and his belief that he had brought shame on his family. For example, we listed on my blackboard the many sacrifices he had made to please his family and the times he went out of his way to help them or provide them with support. These interventions helped Ed to recognize and accept that for the most part, he had been extremely loyal and responsible to his family, even at the expense of his personal happiness. He also recognized that his filial piety was, in part, responsible for the failure of both his marriages. As a result of his new awareness, his feelings of shame and guilt diminished and were replaced with feelings of sadness and hope.

In the ninth and tenth sessions, we closely examined Ed's cultural context and the values he believed in and wished to live by. I continued to use cognitive-restructuring interventions, including reading assignments, to help Ed examine the advantages and disadvantages of both the Chinese and American cultures. Reflecting on his life experiences, he found himself identifying with the issues we discussed in areas such as his inability to reconcile his personal desires with his parents' needs or to face his guilt at the thought of challenging his parents.

Through our discussions, Ed learned that he could live in both the Chinese and American worlds, choosing the best from both. He also learned that his mother's rigid and insensitive behavior was not a reflection of Chinese culture but rather a manifestation of her personality and her own selfish needs. He concluded that he would no longer be governed by her controlling manner and would make decisions about her requests based on what he believed was right and appropriate.

By the twelfth and final session, Ed was still feeling sad about his divorce, but he was also hopeful about his future. Not surprisingly, he had decided to return to San Francisco because he wanted to be close to both his parents and his children. Ed remained a traditionalist in many ways; however, he had achieved family integration and was no longer in an emotional prison. His behaviors and decisions regarding his responsibilities and obligations toward his parents would no longer be based on blind obedience, fear, and shame, but instead on care, freedom, and fairness. Furthermore, Ed felt free to pursue his own personal goals and happiness.

This case describes how CAFT helped Edward Liu achieve family integration by reconciling the differences between his personal desires and his loyalty to his family. Throughout his life, Ed acquiesced to his parents' needs, even though he may have believed that what they asked was unreasonable. Unfortunately, it was only after his second marriage ended that he was able to identify the problem that had plagued him throughout most of his adult life.

Like many first-generation Chinese Americans, Ed was caught between Western culture, which emphasized independence and personal happiness, and Chinese culture, which emphasized interdependency and family loyalty. Through the use of various clinical interventions, I was able to help Ed reconcile his personal desires and the needs of his family. He remained respectful and supportive to his parents and involved with them while at the same time meeting his own personal needs. By integrating the best of Western and Chinese cultures, Ed found peace within himself and with his parents.

Chapter Eleven

"There Is Madness in the Family"

The Ching Family

This chapter tells the story of the Chings, an immigrant family from Hong Kong. The family consisted of Lanny, the father; Connie, his sister; Ronald, age nineteen; Sheryl, age sixteen; Ryan, age fourteen; and Sharon, age thirteen. Mr. Ching and Ronald were born in Hong Kong and his sisters and brother were born in the United States. Mr. Ching worked two jobs, full-time as a stock person and part-time as a waiter, while his sister worked full-time as a house cleaner. When time permitted, the adults socialized with friends and relatives.

From the beginning, the Chings experienced problems in adjusting to their adopted country. In addition to the difficulties they had in accommodating the cultural differences, the adults had difficulty finding work because of their lack of education. In 1992, Mrs. Ching was killed in an automobile accident. Two years later, at the age of eighteen, Ronald suffered a psychotic break. It appeared as though the Chings' dream of finding happiness and prosperity in the United States had turned into a nightmare. This case illustrates how Chinese American Family Therapy can be used to work with a family in which one member suffers from a chronic mental illness and to foster the renewal of lost hopes and aspirations.

The Ching family was referred to the department of mental health for treatment by Ms. Jenkins, Sheryl's school counselor. Ms. Jenkins had been advised by Sheryl's teachers that her school performance had slowly deteriorated during the course of the school year. They also noticed that she was becoming more depressed and socially withdrawn. Initially Sheryl denied that there were any problems. However, during her last meeting with Ms. Jenkins, she broke down and cried hysterically.

Sheryl told Ms. Jenkins that she had been given major household and caretaking responsibilities following her mother's death because her father and aunt had to work. She was able and willing to handle matters until Ryan began associating with delinquent peers and Ronald suffered his psychotic break. As Ronald's condition deteriorated and he became more agitated, Sheryl began to feel more helpless and fearful of his bizarre behaviors. She also began having frequent frightening nightmares. Nevertheless, she was still required to care for Ronald in the absence of her father, her aunt, and a caretaker who had been hired to watch him when she was at school. In addition, her responsibilities at home prohibited her from participating in school activities or socializing with peers.

Mr. Ching refused to seek help for Ronald, attributing his son's problems to fate and evil spirits. He believed that little could be done to change his son's condition and that disclosing the illness to outsiders would be shameful and would lower the family's status in the community. However, Mr. Ching changed his mind and agreed to seek counseling after being told by Ms. Jenkins that Sheryl would become more depressed and her grades would continue to deteriorate unless something was done to rectify the problems at home.

Initial Interview

Present at the initial interview were Mr. Ching, Ronald, and Sheryl. Knowing that Mr. Ching would probably see my questions as prying and being intrusive on his privacy, I made sure that I stayed in the present and did not talk about the family's immigration experiences. I used one of my standard means of joining by briefly sharing with Mr. Ching that my parents were also immigrants and very traditional. I also told him that I had two children and knew the difficulties of raising them.

Mr. Ching was reserved but polite, answering any questions I put to him. He explained that Ms. Jenkins had referred him to counseling because she thought that issues at home were interfering with Sheryl's behavior and school performance. He described Ronald's symptoms, saying that his problems were caused by fate and bad luck. I tried joining with him by indicating that I believed in fate and that I believed it was fate that had brought the family to see me so that I could help turn their luck around. (Chinese are not fatalistic; although they believe in fate, they also believe it can be influenced by several means, including prayer and divine intervention.) Mr. Ching acknowledged that what I said might be true. I explained to Mr. Ching that I needed to take a developmental history in order to make a proper diagnosis of his son's problems. He agreed to my questioning but preferred that Sheryl answer the questions.

Sheryl remembered Ronald's symptoms of mental illness as emerging when he was sixteen. She described him as changing and showing signs of a flat facial expression, scattered thoughts, poor impulse control, and social withdrawal. She said that family members, including herself, were embarrassed at social and cultural engagements because of his inappropriateness. As Ronald's condition worsened, the family hid his problems and their shame regarding him by keeping him out of sight. When Ronald's teachers began expressing concern about his behavior and his drop in school performance, Mr. Ching withdrew him from school, saying that he was being sent to live with an aunt. Instead, he was kept home and confined to his room.

Occasionally, Ronald slipped out of the house and was found disturbing the neighbors. During one such incident, he was reported to the local police by a neighbor who saw him urinating on her flowers. His aunt lied to the investigating officer by telling him that the family would take his advice and obtain professional help, but they continued to hide their shame and embarrassment by confining him and treating him with herbal medicines.

After I took Ronald's developmental history, I socialized and joined with Sheryl by asking about her friends, her interests, and what she enjoyed about school. I then asked her if she agreed with Ms. Jenkins and believed that issues at home were creating problems for her at school, to which she replied yes. In our discussion, Sheryl admitted that she felt like a failure and was guilty and ashamed because of her inability to adequately care for her brothers and because she had disclosed Ronald's mental illness, thereby bringing shame on the family and embarrassing her father by making him come to counseling. Upon hearing this, I told Mr. Ching that he was a lucky man because he had such a loyal, responsible, and obedient daughter. I also praised him for instilling such values in her. I then turned to Sheryl and said that she was also lucky because she had a father who would suffer embarrassment for her sake. I added that he obviously was concerned about her and would do anything to ensure her well-being. (These statements demonstrate the use of positive connotation.) Following my discussion with Sheryl I turned my attention to Ronald.

I joined with Ronald while conducting a mental status evaluation. Based on that evaluation, the description of his premorbid condition, and the description of his behavior at home, it appeared to me that he was suffering from paranoid schizophrenia. His symptoms included disorganized speech, flat affect, persecutory delusions, and auditory hallucinations. From the observations made by his father and Sheryl, it also appeared that his condition was deteriorating, with an increased frequency of anxiety, anger, and argumentativeness.

I shared my initial clinical impressions with Mr. Ching and Sheryl, making it clear that an accurate and thorough assessment would require more time and observations. I explained to Mr. Ching that fate might have caused his son to be inflicted with this problem and that although it might not be curable, with the help of medication and proper treatment, there was a strong likelihood that the illness could be contained and, with assistance, Ronald could live a productive life. I stressed the importance of family support and involvement in the rehabilitation process and emphasized that maximizing his potential for growth would require them to adjust to his needs and abilities. I warned that if he was not treated, Ronald might become violent or suicidal. Fearful of the possibility that his condition would worsen and the impact it was having on

Sheryl, Mr. Ching consented to treatment. I then explained the treatment alternatives.

After planning a collaborative meeting with Dr. Chu, the clinic's psychiatrist, I asked Mr. Ching if there were other problems he would like to discuss. He asked if I would talk to Ryan, who was beginning to create problems at home. This was a sign that he respected me and trusted me with his family. I said I would but indicated that it would be helpful for me to meet all his family, including his sister. Before the session ended, Sheryl disclosed her nightmares and asked if she was going to be like Ronald. I used the cognitive intervention of logical analysis to examine the differences between her and her brother and to assure her that she did not have any of his premorbid symptoms. I said, however, that I was concerned about her nightmares and feelings of guilt, shame, and helplessness. With her father's permission we agreed to address these issues in a subsequent session. I closed the session by reiterating to Mr. Ching what a respectful, obedient, and loyal daughter he had raised and to Sheryl what a courageous and supportive father she had. (Therapists using CAFT recognize that our clients don't remember much that is said in sessions but more often than not will remember what was said last. It is therefore important to end sessions with a statement or information you hope they will retain.)

My diagnostic impression of the Ching family was that Mr. Ching's beliefs and feelings about Ronald's mental illness were normal given his cultural context. Although most families feel that a stigma is attached to mental illness, Chinese Americans, particularly those less acculturated, feel an even greater disgrace in having a mentally ill person in the family. This is due, in part, to their belief that the problem is associated with their child-rearing practices, something they or their ancestors may have done wrong in the past, a hereditary flaw, or a violation of socially sanctioned behaviors. To seek outside help or acknowledge mental illness in the family brings more shame to a family as well as fear of criticism from their extended family and a lessening of status in the community. It is therefore not uncommon for families like the Chings to hide their fear and embarrassment by keeping mentally ill people hidden for years, treating them with herbs, acupuncture, or some other form of Chinese intervention.

Unfortunately, as with Ronald, the pathology of mentally ill people who are kept at home without proper treatment normally worsens until they can no longer be managed by their caretakers. They become either too violent, too bizarre, or self-destructive. At this point, their families are pressured or forced into seeking professional help. With such families, it is extremely important for us to work diligently throughout treatment to alleviate feelings of shame, guilt, and embarrassment and correct any misunderstandings regarding the patient's mental illness and how it can be treated.

In addition to the problem of Ronald's mental illness, it was evident that Sheryl was an overburdened, parentified child who had been given too much responsibility and authority and not enough support to effectively handle an older brother with a serious mental disorder and a younger one who was beginning to exhibit oppositional behavior. The family's problems consisted of a need for situational adjustment (adjusting to mental illness) and developmental adjustment (helping a young boy entering adolescence who is seeking his identity). Left untreated, these problems could lead to a serious breakdown of family functioning.

The initial intervention was aimed at providing treatment for Ronald. This would not only help him but also reduce Sheryl's fear and stress level. The remaining tasks were to develop a comprehensive treatment plan for Ronald and his family, make Sheryl's parental and household responsibilities manageable, dissipate Sheryl's negative feelings toward herself, and prevent Ryan from continuing to exhibit oppositional behaviors.

Subsequent Sessions

In the second session, Mr. Ching, Sheryl, Ronald, and I met with Dr. Chu, who examined Ronald and started him on psychotropic medication. She explained to the family how the medication worked, its possible side effects, and the need for blood tests. She also stressed the importance of monitoring Ronald's adjustment to the medication. In the second segment of the session, I continued to help the family understand the nature of Ronald's disease and how they could be involved in his recovery and adjustment. We also examined programs that could aid him in his rehabilitation and continued growth. (He eventually was admitted into a transitional program for young adults.) I closed the session by giving the family literature in both English and Chinese on understanding schizophrenia and its treatment.

Mr. Ching brought his other two children, Sharon and Ryan, to the third session. His sister didn't attend, believing that it was unnecessary. After asking about Ronald's condition during the week, I joined with them by asking about their friends, interests, and goals. In our discussion, Ryan mentioned that he wanted to own a Porsche like one he had seen in the parking lot. I told him that it was mine and, following the session, I took him out to look at and sit in it. (This intervention served to join with him and provide him with an incentive to be successful.) I then gave Ryan a pep talk and told him that I knew of many Chinese rags-to-riches stories and that I believed he could be one of them.

I explained to the two adolescents my purpose in having them attend the session. After exploring their understanding of Ronald's problem, I shared information on schizophrenia and told them what they could do to help. I then told Ryan that his father had some concerns regarding his behavior, and Mr. Ching was asked to state them. He said that Ryan was acting disrespectfully, not obeying Sheryl, associating with bad kids, and beginning to do poorly in school. I asked Ryan to respond to his father's comments, to which he replied that he had nothing to say. (I purposely did not ask for his perceptions of the problems, which would have put him on an equal footing with his father.) Respecting Mr. Ching's request, I spoke with Ryan alone.

My clinical impression of Ryan was that although he tried to give the appearance of being tough, characterologically he was flexible, sensitive, and caring. He was also intelligent, perceptive, and insightful. In speaking with him, I tried to put his father's criticism in a positive frame by explaining the importance of his father's request (something his father would be unaccustomed to doing) and by saying that his father was concerned about his well-being. I also told him that as a parent, I would make the same request. I asked if he believed that his father was concerned about him, to which he said yes. I then asked if he believed that his father's request was unreasonable. (The metamessage in this line of questioning was that I was concerned about his views and willing to listen to them.) He replied that he didn't like the fact that his sister tried to boss him around. He also thought he should be able to choose his friends and said that although two of them had been arrested for car theft, it wasn't something he would ever do. Finally, he said that he found school boring. I told him that if he was willing, we would address these issues with his father. I also said that I would be willing to meet with his teachers to try to make his classes more interesting. He agreed to talk with his father but said that he would think about my going to his school.

After continuing to speak with Ryan about his interests and hopes for the future, I met with him and his father alone. (This was done to create a father-son subgroup and to make it more comfortable for Ryan to speak. With my encouragement, Ryan told his father what he had shared with me. His father responded in a reasonable manner, explaining to me his concern for his son. After having Ryan acknowledge his father's positive intent, I spoke with Mr. Ching alone. (I didn't want to educate him in front of his son.)

I explained to Mr. Ching that it was common for younger children, particularly boys, not to want to be told what to do by an older sibling. I also explained the importance of having the authority over the children remain with him and not Sheryl. He could accomplish this by telling Ryan and Sharon what he expected them to do and how to behave when he or their aunt was not at home. If they did not comply with what was expected, he would be the person who would discipline them. Sheryl's duties would be to remind them of their responsibilities and report to their father any misconduct. This would shift Sheryl's role from that of a parent to that of an older child who was supporting the wishes of her father. It would also lighten Sheryl's burden at home and take her out of the position of being perceived by Ryan as bossy. Finally, Ryan would be directly accountable to his father rather than his sister.

To further relieve Sheryl's burden at home and to allow her time to socialize with friends, I suggested to Mr. Ching that if possible, he extend the caretaker's time by two hours, two days a week. I went on to explain the importance of socializing for Sheryl. After some discussion, Mr. Ching agreed with my recommendations.

When they returned to the session, the children were told of the changes. I highlighted the fact that the changes were being made because their father wanted what he thought was best for them. The children asked for several points of clarification. Both Sheryl and Ryan were pleased with the changes.

By the fourth session, the progress was evident. Ronald was less agitated, Sheryl was not feeling as overwhelmed and was doing better at school, and Ryan was more cooperative at home. Mr. Ching had received a letter from Ms. Jenkins (which I had asked her to send), informing him that Sheryl was doing better at school. I asked Mr. Ching if he believed that his luck was changing, to which he laughed and replied yes.

The fourth through sixth sessions were focused on continuing to monitor Ronald's response to the medication, helping the family adapt to and provide support for Ronald's needs and working with Sheryl and Ryan to resolve minor conflicts. I spent part of the fifth session with Sheryl alone, working to normalize her negative feelings and using cognitive-restructuring interventions to help her to recognize her positive attributes, including being responsible, obedient, and loyal. In the sixth session, I asked Ryan if he wanted me to accompany him and his father to school to work with his teacher. He declined my offer, saying that his grades were slowly improving. I suspect that my offering to go to school with him was an impetus for him to do better. He probably preferred to improve his grades rather than risk the embarrassment of having his father and me meet with his teachers and possibly be seen by his peers.

By the seventh meeting (this was the ninth week from the date treatment began, because the family had to miss two sessions), it was evident that the Chings had achieved a high level of family integration. Ronald's medication was very effective at controlling his symptoms, the family had devised a plan to help contain his behavior at home, and they were no longer afraid to take him out in public. Ronald was enrolled in a young adults' transitional program and was planning to attend self-help group meetings. Sheryl no longer had nightmares and once again felt comfortable handling household responsibilities. Finally, Ryan was cooperative and respectful at home and reported that his grades were improving. Mr. Ching agreed to have the family continue to meet with me on a monthly basis for consultation. This was important for observing and assessing Ronald's mental illness so that an accurate diagnosis and prognosis for his illness could be made.

This case demonstrates a typical response of many Chinese to having a mentally ill family member. Like the Chings, feeling ashamed and disgraced, they hide the mentally ill person until the psychopathology becomes so severe that they must seek professional help. Using cognitive and supportive interventions, I assisted Mr. Ching in overcoming his shameful feelings. I also assisted the family in treating Ronald's schizophrenia properly, relieving Sheryl's feelings of being overwhelmed, and correcting Ryan's oppositional behavior. In so doing, I enabled the Chings to achieve family integration.

Chapter Twelve

Mental Health and Social Services

Current Status and Challenges
for the Future

The previous chapters described Chinese American Family Therapy, including its evolution and application to various problems. This final chapter will present a brief historical overview of the human service needs of Chinese Americans and the efforts by individuals, groups, and organizations to meet them. It will also present demographics on Chinese Americans and the conclusions that can be drawn from this information. In addition, it will look at the current status of mental health, child and adolescent welfare, and adult social services provided to Chinese Americans, including issues related to utilization, staffing, and funding. Finally, the chapter will discuss the future challenges faced by human service professionals working with Chinese Americans.

The ideas articulated in the chapter are derived from my personal observations; a review of professional mental health, child welfare, and social service literature; and interviews with Asian American mental health and social service administrators and counselors in Los Angeles, Alameda, and San Francisco counties in California. Although I am most familiar with the mental health and social service delivery systems in California, I believe that what is reflected in this chapter is applicable to other areas of the country with large concentrations of Chinese Americans, such as New York City, Boston, and Chicago.

Historical Overview of the Human Service
Needs of Chinese Americans

As indicated in Chapter One, the articulation and eventual recog-nition of the mental health, child welfare, and social service needs of Chinese Americans were intricately involved in the Asian Amer-ican movement, which began in the early 1960s. The pioneers spearheading this movement included National Institute of Mental Health representatives Patrick Okura and Ford Kuramoto, agency executives George Nishinaka and Joyce Law, and researchers William T. Liu, Stanley Sue, and Derald Wing Sue. Others in the forefront were the writers Betty L. Sung, Bok-Lim Kim, and Fran-cis L. K. Hsu; the educators Harry Kitano, Evelyn Lee, and Kenji Murase; and the practitioners Royal Morales, Paul Chikasawa, and Pei Nor Chin. Without these and the many other Asians and non-Asians involved at the beginning of the Asian American move-ment, the human service needs of Chinese Americans wouldn't be being met today.

The social and political climate of the 1960s and 1970s was one of liberalism, optimism, social change, and experimentation. The focus of the time was on civil rights, equal opportunity for ethnic minorities in the workplace, and the establishment of ethnic and racial pride, as well as on trying to meet the social, welfare, and mental health needs of the elderly, poor, underserved, and disen-franchised. Social service and mental health programs were inclu-sive, trying to serve all those needing assistance. The definition of mental illness, for example, was broadly interpreted, allowing men-tal health professionals to serve more than just the chronically mentally ill.

Throughout the 1960s and early 1970s, a number of important changes took place in the fields of mental health and social service. Unemployed parents were included in Aid to Families with De-pendent Children payments in states that elected to include them. The 1963 Mental Retardation Facilities and Community Mental Health Centers Construction Act was passed to deinstitutionalize mental illness and establish a mental health system that ensured continuity of care for the chronically mentally ill. The Great Society programs were launched, which established such organizations as the Job Corps, Operation Head Start, Volunteers in Service to America, the Neighborhood Youth Corps, and Food Stamps. In 1972, the Supplemental Security Income Program was enacted, which combined and federalized public assistance for the adult poor, aged, blind, and disabled.

Also significant was the passing of the Immigration and Nationality Act of 1965. This act abolished national-origin quotas, the first step toward removing discrimination against Chinese immigration. China was no longer restricted to a quota of 105, but instead was entitled, like other countries, to 20,000 immigrants. As a result, Chinese, along with other Asians and Pacific Islanders, have made up over a third of all legal immigrants to the United States since 1970.

During the 1960s and 1970s, significant federal money was available from the U.S. Department of Mental Health to fund research projects, training and demonstration programs, and graduate education. In fact, my master's degree was funded by a National Child Welfare Grant and my doctorate by a scholarship awarded by the National Institute of Mental Health. It was during this "War on Poverty" period that attention was first directed toward identifying the human service needs of Chinese Americans.

Prior to this time, Chinese were considered to be a model minority, taking care of ourselves and needing no mental health, child welfare, or social services. The first challenge to the leaders in the Asian American movement was to dispel this myth. Although some in the general public still think that we have no problems, I believe that this challenge has been met. Through education, advocacy, and research, elected officials at all levels of government and mental health, child welfare, and social service providers have recognized that Chinese, as well as all the other Asian American groups, have difficulties and are in need of both publicly and privately supported human services. This is reflected in the range of programs and services that are aimed directly at meeting the following problems faced by Chinese Americans:

1. Mental illness
2. Developmental disability
3. Child abuse and neglect
4. Juvenile delinquency and gang violence
5. Domestic violence
6. Divorce
7. Drug and alcohol abuse
8. AIDS
9. Poor housing
10. Unemployment

To effectively meet the needs of traditional Chinese Americans, it is important for agencies and clinics to be staffed with competent bilingual and bicultural professionals. The second challenge for the early Asian American leaders was to recruit, educate, and train such individuals into the mental health and social service professions. By working with graduate schools of social work and psychology and encouraging them to recruit and retain Chinese American faculty and students, their efforts have been successful. Prior to the 1960s, with the exception of medicine, very few Chinese Americans entered human services; instead, they opted to enter the fields of pure science. Since that time, however, the number of social workers and psychologists has increased steadily. Today, many programs and facilities that serve Chinese Americans have adequate bilingual and bicultural staff.

Although significant gains have been made during the past thirty-five years in defining and meeting the needs of Chinese Americans, there is still a great deal more to do. However, today's social and political climate is significantly altered from that of the 1960s, presenting new and different challenges to those of us in the human service field. Today we are in a conservative social and political climate where the poor, especially those on public welfare, are again being criticized, scapegoated, and blamed for the economic and social ills of the time. The emphasis in human service is on cost containment, with programs and services being restrictive rather than inclusive. The definition of mental illness is narrowly interpreted; consequently, public mental health programs are limited to serving the chronically mentally ill. In addition, there is an anti-immigration sentiment that is reflected in a significant increase in hate crimes against Asian Americans and the recent attempt by Congress to pass federal welfare legislation that would drastically reduce benefits for legal immigrants.

The responsibility for caring for the poor and disenfranchised has shifted from the federal government to the individual states. As a result, little money is available for anything other than direct services. Many are calling the present period the "war on the poor." In this conservative social and political arena, the mental health, child welfare, and social service needs of Chinese Americans are on the rise. This is the result of the large influx of new immigrants, outreach efforts on the part of mental health and social service professionals, programs that have been established to serve the needs of Chinese Americans, and the willingness of more individuals and families to seek services on a volunteer basis. The major challenge for us in the Asian American movement today, therefore, is to find the funding and resources to meet these growing needs.

Demographics

The influx of Chinese immigrants changed dramatically with the enactment of the Immigration and Nationality Act of 1965. Since that time, there has been a steady growth in the number of Chinese entering the United States. However, unlike my parents' immigration in the 1930s, when most Chinese were from southeast China near Hong Kong, the newer waves of immigration arrive from other parts of China as well as from other parts of the world, especially

Taiwan, Hong Kong, and Vietnam. This section will present demographics on Chinese Americans related to population distribution, age composition, education, English proficiency, economic status, and marital status, and the conclusions that can be drawn from this information.

Table 12.1 shows the concentration of the Chinese population in 1960 and 1990. The number of Chinese in the United States grew from 237,292 to 1,645,472, nearly seven times, in thirty years. The concentration of Chinese Americans continues to remain constant in a few states, but there has been a substantial increase in New Jersey, Massachusetts, and Illinois. The largest concentration of Chinese in the six states, listed in Table 12.1, is not surprising. First, immigration among Chinese tends to be a family affair. A new immigrant sends for his wife and children, and the family is reunited under one roof. If brothers, sisters, parents, or cousins are brought over, the newcomers want to stay close to their relatives, not only because of family connections but also because, in the beginning, new immigrants must often depend upon family members who immigrated previously for a job or for support. Between 1990 and 1995, 133,726 or 34 percent of the 391,693 Chinese who immigrated from either Taiwan, China, or Hong Kong located in California (*Statistical Yearbook of the Immigration and Naturalization Service, 1990–1995*).

Second, the six states in which Chinese have concentrated have all established Chinese neighborhoods or "Chinatowns" in their major cities. New arrivals, particularly those who have little education and are on the lower end of the socioeconomic scale, wish to live in an environment that is familiar, and therefore they move into or live close to these Chinese enclaves. In these communities, Chinese is spoken, cultural events are celebrated, and Chinese groceries and furnishings are easily purchased.

Third, Chinese communities allow recent immigrants, particularly those who don't speak English, to find employment or start small businesses. Unfortunately, many of the newly arriving immigrants are exploited and find themselves working for less than minimum wage in substandard working conditions.

Table 12.1. Concentration of Chinese Population in the United States, 1960 and 1990.

| State | 1960 | | 1990 | |
	Population	Percent of Total Chinese Population	Population	Percent of Total Chinese population
California	95,600	40	704,850	43
New York	37,573	16	284,144	17
Hawaii	38,197	16	68,804	4
New Jersey	3,813	2	59,084	4
Massachusetts	6,745	3	53,792	3
Illinois	7,047	3	49,936	3
Other states	48,317	20	424,862	26
Total	237,292	100	1,645,472	100

Source: Adapted from "Asians in America," 1991, p. 6, and Sung, 1967, p. 112.

The concentration of Chinese in certain areas makes it easier to deliver culturally sensitive health, mental health, and social services. The Chinatown Service Center in Los Angeles, for example, is located in the middle of Chinatown, as is Asian Community Mental Health Services in Oakland. Both provide a full range of services and are staffed by bilingual and bicultural Chinese staff.

The 1990 census reveals that the large majority of Chinese Americans are immigrants. Of the 1,648,000 Chinese in the United States, 488,000 or 30 percent are native-born, whereas 1,160,000 or 70 percent were born elsewhere. It also reveals that among the immigrant group, 742,400 or 64 percent speak English well or very well. Thus, although a significant number of Chinese immigrants in need of mental health or social services will require a Chinese-speaking therapist, the majority can be served by English-speaking clinicians if necessary.

Table 12.2 shows the age composition of native-born and immigrant Chinese. Of the native-born Chinese, 287,920 or 59 percent are nineteen years of age or younger, 170,800 or 35 percent are between twenty and fifty-nine years of age, and 29,280 or 6 percent

Table 12.2. Age Composition of Native-Born
and Immigrant Chinese Americans.

| | Native-Born | | Immigrant | |
Age	Population	Percent of Chinese	Population	Percent of Chinese
0–9	185,440	38	34,800	3
10–19	102,480	21	127,600	11
20–29	68,320	14	232,000	20
30–39	58,560	12	290,000	25
40–49	29,280	6	197,200	17
50–59	14,640	3	127,600	11
60–69	14,640	3	92,800	8
70–79	9,760	2	46,400	4
80+	4,880	1	11,600	1
Total	488,000	100	1,160,000	100

Source: Adapted from Hing and Lee, 1996, pp. 46, 48.

are sixty years of age or older. Of the immigrant group, 162,400 or 14 percent are nineteen years of age or younger, 846,800 or 73 percent are between twenty and fifty-nine years of age, and 150,800 or 13 percent are sixty years of age or older. Thus, the large majority of Chinese Americans are foreign-born and between the ages of twenty and fifty-nine. There are also a significant number of foreign-born Chinese sixty years of age or older, many of whom, according to studies, are in need of mental health and social services.

Table 12.3 shows educational attainment among Chinese Americans. Among Chinese Americans twenty-five years of age or older, 76 percent of native-born Chinese Americans and 56 percent of immigrants have at least some college education, whereas 8 percent of native-born Chinese Americans and 29 percent of immigrants have less than a high school education. These figures are not surprising. It is well known that Chinese value education. Consequently when they are given the opportunity, they take it. Unfortu-

**Table 12.3. Educational Attainment Among
Chinese Americans Twenty-Five Years of Age or Older.**

	Native-Born (percent)	Immigrant (percent)
Less than high school	8	29
High school diploma	16	15
Some college	25	17
Bachelor's degree	33	20
Master's degree	11	13
Doctorate/professional	7	6
Total	100	100

Source: Adapted from Hing and Lee, 1996, p. 50.

nately, many Chinese immigrants did have not have the opportunity to receive an education in their country of origin. However, some, like my parents, did have this opportunity, and they encouraged their children to take advantage of the educational opportunities in this country and to seek advanced degrees.

Table 12.4 shows the economic status of Chinese Americans, including labor-force participation, unemployment, poverty, and category of public assistance. As shown in the table, in 1990 a large segment of Chinese immigrants, 185,600 or 16 percent, lived in poverty and 104,400 or 9 percent received public assistance. These statistics dispel the myth that all Chinese Americans are successful, are financially secure, and do not need public assistance.

Table 12.5 indicates the marital status of Chinese Americans. Immigrants have a high rate of marriage and both native-born Chinese Americans and immigrants have a low rate of divorce. The following list summarizes the data:

1. A large number of Chinese arrived in the United States following the Immigration and Nationality Act of 1965.

2. The majority of Chinese Americans, 70 percent, are immigrants.

**Table 12.4. Economic Status of Native-Born
and Immigrant Chinese Americans.**

	Native-Born Population	Percent	Immigrant Population	Percent
People in the labor force	331,840	68	754,000	65
Unemployed	14,640	3	34,800	3
People in poverty	39,040	8	185,600	16
People receiving public assistance	9,760	2	58,000	5
Poor receiving public assistance	19,520	4	104,400	9

Source: Abstracted from Hing and Lee, 1996, p. 52.

3. Chinese immigrants are a diverse group and come from various countries.

4. The overwhelming majority of Chinese are concentrated in six states, with 43 percent residing in California in 1990.

5. Nearly 65 percent of immigrants can speak English well or very well.

6. Nearly 75 percent of immigrants are between the ages of twenty and fifty-nine; however, a significant number are over sixty.

7. The educational level attained is higher among native-born Chinese; however, over 55 percent of immigrants have some college experience.

8. A significant number of immigrants have less than a high school education.

9. The unemployment rate for both native-born Chinese Americans and immigrants is relatively low; however, a significant number of immigrants live in poverty and receive public assistance.

Table 12.5. Marital Status of Chinese Americans
Eighteen Years of Age or Older.

	Native-Born Population	Percent	Immigrant Population	Percent
Married	214,720	44	777,200	67
Widowed	14,640	3	58,000	5
Divorced	24,400	5	34,800	3
Separated	4,880	1	11,600	1
Never married	229,360	47	278,400	24
Total	488,000	100	1,160,000	100

Source: Adapted from Hing and Lee, 1996, p. 49.

10. The mean income for immigrants is significantly lower than that of native-born Chinese Americans.

11. The divorce rate among both native-born Chinese Americans and immigrants is low.

Given these findings and what is already known, six conclusions are warranted. First, native-born Chinese appear to be successful. Overall, they achieve a high level of education, are employed, and have a good median income. They also have a low rate of divorce and, both by percentage and in actual numbers, few receive public assistance. This does not mean, of course, that all native-born people are problem-free. Some do fall into low income categories, with problems of poverty, low occupational attainment, and reliance on public welfare.

Second, immigrant Chinese tend to fall into two distinct groups. There are those who do well; they achieve a high level of education, are skilled, become employed or own businesses, and earn a good medium income. Others do very poorly; they may be uneducated, unskilled, unemployed, living below the poverty line, and dependent on public assistance. In some households several adults must work at low-paying jobs to survive. In other cases, at-risk elderly live in isolation without emotional or family support.

Third, in the past, poor Chinese immigrants were able to overcome adversity and achieve success on their own through self-sacrifice, mutual support, and diligence. This is reflected in part by the success of their offspring. In today's more complex political, social, economic, and highly scientific and technological environment, however, many poor immigrants also need the assistance of public and private agencies and organizations to overcome their problems and fulfill their hopes and dreams.

Fourth, the large majority of Chinese Americans speak English; therefore, non-Chinese therapists can work with this population. It is, however, important that they be familiar with the customs and traditions of the Chinese culture.

Fifth, the divorce rate among Chinese immigrants is 3 percent, much lower than the 1994 national divorce rate of 17 percent (U.S. Bureau of the Census, 1995). However, this 3 percent represents thirty-four thousand people, a significant number, and everyone I spoke with believed that divorce among Chinese immigrants is rising quickly. This is due in part to Chinese women, who refuse to remain in an abusive or exploitative marriage when they are given support and an alternative.

Sixth, Chinese Americans, both native-born and immigrants, still place great value on education, family cohesion, and diligence. They work hard, pay their taxes, and contribute to the progress and well-being of this society. Through the years, they have continued to move from being outsiders to joining the American mainstream. There is nothing to suggest that they will not continue to do so.

In this section we looked at the general demographic information on Chinese Americans. Now we will begin to look at their particular needs and how they are being addressed.

Mental Health Services

Since the early 1960s, great strides have been made in meeting the needs of mentally ill Chinese. The 1963 Mental Retardation Facilities and Community Mental Health Centers Construction Act established the mental health center as the primary locus of community care for mentally ill people. Today, as in the past, centers or departments fulfill the following objectives:

1. Replacing institutional care with care in the community
2. Providing services to the entire community and not just patients
3. Planning services for the mental health of the entire community
4. Providing continuity of care directed toward the least restrictive settings for care

To achieve their objectives, centers or departments provide five essential services: emergency services, outpatient care, partial hospitalization, inpatient care for acute situations, and the community services of consultation and education. In addition, long-term hospitalization in state-operated facilities, residential treatment programs, psychosocial rehabilitation services, and board and care homes are considered to be an integral part of providing both quality and continuity of care to mentally ill clients.

Overcoming Underutilization

As indicated previously, Chinese Americans, particularly those who are less assimilated into American culture, have historically underutilized mental health services. This has been attributed to their medical beliefs, the stigma attached to having someone in the family who is mentally ill, the shame attached to seeking help outside the family, and a tradition of self-reliance. Although these are contributing factors, one study involving residents of San Francisco's Chinese community indicates that underutilization is not the result of an unwillingness to admit to symptoms or to the use of alternative cultural sources of help, but rather to a lack of knowledge about existing services and ignorance about mental illness and its treatment (Loo, Tong, and True, 1989).

Through research and experience, we know how to attract mentally ill immigrant Chinese to treatment as well as how to retain them. First, we must reach out to the community, through either gatekeepers or established organizations, and educate the residents regarding mental illness, its treatment, and the availability of services. This can be done in conjunction with a public relations program, using talk shows and advertising on the radio and in newspapers. Outreach efforts must be a continual process, not a one-time effort. Second, our facilities should be located in the community, where clients have easy access to them. Third, our facilities must be user-friendly. This includes having flexible hours and allowing clients to drop in or call on the telephone, using Chinese decor, having support staff who speak Chinese, and distributing educational materials written in Chinese; it may also include serving refreshments and celebrating cultural events. Fourth, we should have bilingual and bicultural therapists. Fifth, we must have sensitive and competent therapists. Sixth, when possible, we should provide a full array of services and programs; they often supplement one another. Finally, we should combine cultural interventions with Western practices. For example, to establish a support group with his chronically mentally ill patients, a psychologist at one of the Chinese serving clinics in Los Angeles initially served lunch to his patients each month while they waited to receive medications from the staff psychiatrist. They talked and socialized while they ate. Following lunch, they participated in Chinese physical exercises. After a while, his patients insisted that he no longer continue serving them but remain for the group sessions.

Los Angeles, Alameda, and San Francisco counties in California do very well in providing services to Chinese and other Asian American groups. The mental health departments in the three counties are similar in that their target groups are organized according to age: children and adolescents (from birth to age seventeen), adults (from eighteen to fifty-nine), and, for Los Angeles and San Francisco, older adults (over sixty). The three counties are also similar in that their services to Chinese are under the umbrella of

"Asian American"; therefore, clinics aimed at serving Chinese are also set up to serve other Asian American groups. Given their small numbers and diversification, targeting each Asian group would be far too impractical.

The three counties are different in the way they organize and deliver their services to the Chinese community. The delivery systems are based on the county's size and geography and where the Chinese population is concentrated. Los Angeles, for example, is an extremely large county, both in population and in area. Although Chinese are dispersed throughout the county, large concentrations live in the downtown Chinatown area, the San Gabriel Valley, and Long Beach. Compared to Los Angeles, San Francisco is small, both geographically and in the number of Chinese residents. Although there is a large concentration of Chinese in the downtown Chinatown area, they, along with other Asian Americans, are highly visible throughout the entire city and county. This is due to the fact that Asian Americans represent nearly 30 percent of the county's population.

Los Angeles County

The Los Angeles County Department of Mental Health designates eight service areas that cover the entire county. Delivery of services is provided by the county's own mental health facilities, nongovernment agencies, and private nonprofit organizations. Table 12.6 shows the population of Los Angeles County by race or ethnicity in 1990; clients served by the Los Angeles County Department of Mental Health by race or ethnicity, fiscal year 1995–96; and Department of Mental Health clinical staff by race or ethnicity, fiscal year 1995–96. In 1990 there were 8,863,164 Los Angeles County residents, of whom 954,485 or nearly 11 percent were Asian Americans and Pacific Islanders. Of these, 245,033 or nearly 26 percent were of Chinese ancestry (*Asians in America*, 1991; "Los Angeles County Cultural Competency Needs Assessment," 1997). The number of Asian American clients was 9,022, representing 5

Table 12.6. Population of Los Angeles County, Clients Served by Los Angeles County Department of Mental Health, and Department of Mental Health Clinical Staff, by Race or Ethnicity.

Race or Ethnicity	Population of Los Angeles County		Department of Mental Health Clients		Department of Mental Health Clinical Staff	
	Number	Percent	Number	Percent	Number	Percent
Caucasian	5,035,103	57	66,162	39	3,180	52
African American	992,974	11	36,609	22	1,149	19
Asian American	954,485	11	9,022	5	711	12
Native American	45,508	0	537		34	1
Other	1,835,094	21	18,219	11	245	4
Hispanic	3,351,242[a]	NA	38,742	23	819	13
Total	8,863,164	100	169,291	100	6,138	100

Source: Los Angeles County Department of Mental Health, Program Support Bureau, Planning and Management Information Systems, 1997.

percent of the county's client population served by all county and noncounty facilities. There were 711 Asian American clinical staff (this figure excludes fee-for-service providers but includes contract agency employees), representing 12 percent of the employees who provide clinical services.

Conclusions cannot be drawn about the utilization of services by Chinese Americans using the statistics in Table 12.6 because the clients served are designated as Asian and not Chinese. More than likely, a disproportionate number of Asian groups other than Chinese use these services. It is also difficult to ascertain whether or not Asian Americans in general are underutilizing services. We can compare the percentage of Asian Americans residing in Los Angeles County (11 percent) with the percentage of clients being served (5 percent) and conclude that Asian Americans are being underserved. We do not know if 11 percent of the Asian American population needs mental health services; however, we can conclude from the statistics that the ratio of Asian American clinical staff in the system (12 percent) to Asian Americans being served (5 percent) is high. This is an indication that the county is committed to serving Chinese and other Asian Americans.

Another indicator of the county's commitment is the hiring of bilingual staff. In fiscal year 1995–96, 53 Cantonese-speaking staff were available to serve 589 Medi-Cal-eligible Cantonese-speaking clients.

Still another sign of the county's commitment to Chinese is the fact that the facilities serving Chinese and other Asian American groups are strategically placed to reach out, serve, and provide easy access to potential clients. The Coastal Asian Pacific Mental Health Service is an example of such a facility. It was established in 1984 to provide a full range of mental health programs to the chronically mentally ill of all ages and their family members in the South Bay–Gardena area of Los Angeles County. Their 1990 figures indicate that 10.2 percent of the clients served were Asian Americans.

Finally, another demonstration of the county's desire to provide services to Chinese Americans is its willingness to contract with private nonprofit agencies that have a history of providing quality services. Such an agency is Pacific Clinics, founded in 1926 as the Pasadena Child Guidance Clinic. In 1986, the agency was awarded a mental health contract that established the Asian Pacific Family Center in the San Gabriel Valley, the largest, most intensively Chinese settlement within southern California. Since its inception, the agency has grown enormously, providing numerous services and programs, including

- School-based mental health programs
- Asian Communities Together to Improve Our Neighborhood, a comprehensive substance abuse–prevention program for Asian youth
- A comprehensive Asian youth and family enhancement program to help improve the relationship between children and parents
- A child abuse–prevention program

- Skills training for Chinese parents
- School, Center, Law Enforcement, a delinquency-prevention program

During the 1994–95 fiscal year, the Asian Pacific Family Center served over fourteen thousand clients, of whom 46 percent were Chinese, 30 percent Vietnamese, 12 percent Japanese, 9 percent Korean, 10 percent Filipino, 1 percent Cambodian, and 1 percent other. The vast majority of the Center's clients (92 percent) are low-income, with over half of the client population (78 percent) paying for services through Medi-Cal. These statistics and their programs indicate that the Center serves a vital role in meeting the mental health needs of Asian American groups, particularly the Chinese.

Beyond the essential services provided by the Los Angeles County Department of Mental Health and its provider network, the other services essential to providing continuity of care for chronically mentally ill Chinese (board and care, residential treatment, and long-term hospitalization) are lacking. This is true not only for Los Angeles but for San Francisco and Alameda counties as well. Very few licensed board and care homes have personnel who speak Chinese or provide a culturally sensitive environment. Consequently, it is extremely difficult, if not impossible, to place Chinese mental health clients in need of such support.

Only one long-term residential treatment program serves the Asian American chronically ill population in Los Angeles County; this is the Asian Pacific Residential Treatment Program, located in West Los Angeles in a heavily populated African American community. The program has a sixty-four-bed capacity. It offers a culturally sensitive living environment with bilingual and bicultural staff. In addition to its residency program, it provides a number of other services, including case management, medication dispersement, and an English as a Second Language program. It also has an outpatient component that serves chronically mentally ill Asian clients. More of such programs are certainly needed.

Los Angeles County contracts with Metropolitan State Hospital for beds to serve severely disturbed mentally ill clients needing long-term care. Within the hospital is an Asian unit that has bilingual and bicultural therapists. The unit attempts to provide a culturally sensitive environment by, among other things, allowing families to bring home-cooked food, celebrating cultural holidays, having Asian decor, and providing educational material in Asian languages. However, Asian patients spend an inordinate amount of time in the hospital (the average length of stay is three and a half years, but some remain over ten), leaving no room for others to enter. Often clients have no place to go or inadequate collaborative work is done with community agencies to facilitate their return to the community.

To rectify this problem, the Asian Pacific Policy and Planning Council, an umbrella organization involving numerous human service organizations that serve the Asian American community, has submitted a proposal to the Los Angeles County Department of Mental Health entitled *Asian Pacific Islander Partners Intensive Case Management Project* (*API Partners Project*). The proposal outlines a program that will foster the movement of clients out of Metropolitan State Hospital. The program requires the cooperation of seven community-based and public organizations (Asian Pacific Counseling and Treatment Center, Asian Pacific Family Center, Asian Pacific Residential Treatment, Coastal Asian Pacific Mental Health, Long Beach Asian Pacific Mental Health, Tri-Cities Mental Health, and Western Region Asian Pacific), dispersed throughout Los Angeles County and experienced in the delivery of mental health services. To effectively achieve the proposed overall goal, API Partners Project proposes to become an integral participant in the admission, treatment, and discharge planning for all Asian American and Pacific Islander patients at Metropolitan State Hospital. This is seen as critical to sustain the long-term impact on cost reduction and the clinically effective use of hospital-based resources for acutely and severely ill clients. If it is successful, the project will be a model for use in other counties and states.

Through the strategic placement of its own clinics, the use of community-based multiservice agencies, an abundance of bilingual and bicultural staff, and its commitment to serve ethnic minority groups, the Los Angeles Department of Mental Health appears to be meeting the needs of the Chinese mentally ill. Unfortunately, as indicated previously, much more is needed in the areas of culturally sensitive board and care facilities, residential treatment programs, and long-term hospitalization.

San Francisco County

In 1990, the population of San Francisco County was 723,959, with 210,876 or 29.13 percent being Asian Americans and 127,140 or 17.56 percent being of Chinese ancestry (*Asians in America*, 1991, p. 45). The San Francisco Division of Mental Health and Substance Abuse Services under the Department of Public Health provides mental health services in its own clinics, which are located throughout the city. The Chinatown/North Beach clinic, located a few blocks away from the heart of Chinatown, provides both outpatient and day treatment services and is staffed by bilingual and bicultural Chinese-speaking therapists. Their fiscal year 1996–97 statistical report showed that 92 or 63.45 percent of their day treatment patients and 732 or 44.10 percent of their outpatient clients were Chinese Americans, most of whom suffered from mood or thought disorders, such as major depression, bipolar disorder, schizophrenia, and paranoia. The success of the clinic in meeting the mental health needs of Chinatown residents is the result of its location, consumer-friendly atmosphere, competent bilingual and bicultural staff, and history of reaching out and educating community residents.

In addition to its own facilities, the Division of Mental Health and Substance Abuse Services also has contracts with other organizations to provide both essential and special services; for example, the staff of the Comprehensive Child Crisis Service Center respond immediately to children in crisis, and the Richmond Area

Multiservices Center has the objective of providing a full range of mental health services to the Asian American community. Both centers are staffed primarily by bilingual and bicultural Asian Americans.

Another agency serving the mental health needs of the Chinese community is the Chinatown Child Development Center, founded in 1973. Initially funded under a grant from the National Institute of Mental Health, this clinic is now supported by the City and County of San Francisco. Its target population is children under fourteen years of age and their families who meet the admission criteria for mental health services. It provides a full range of clinical services and has several satellite clinics based in various elementary and middle schools. Sixty-five percent of the Center's clientele are Chinese.

The mental health network of agencies in San Francisco is a comprehensive and integrated system that reaches out to and educates the communities it serves, allows easy access for its clients, and provides a full range of essential and specialized services. It is flexible, letting clients select the facility in which they wish to receive services. Thus, Chinese-speaking clients always have access to bilingual and bicultural therapists and specialized services.

Alameda County

There are 1,279,182 residents of Alameda County, of whom 192,554 or 15.05 percent are Asian American, with 68,585 or 5.36 being of Chinese ancestry. The county's mental health programs are under the direction of its Behavioral Health Care and Alcohol and Drug Services. The services are delivered primarily through contract agencies (60 percent) and serve all ethnic groups. This extensive contracting of services provides tremendous flexibility in addressing the needs of the county's mentally ill.

Asian Community Mental Health Services (ACMHS), one of Alameda County's largest contract agencies, is located in Oakland's Chinatown. It was established in 1974 to fill the void in mental health care for the Asian Pacific community. The founding members were concerned about the well-being of the Asian family; they wanted children to thrive in supportive environments and adults to develop their potential as fully as possible.

ACMHS is unusual because its clinical services are provided by therapists both with and without master's degrees. This is a result of the insufficient number of bilingual and bicultural Asian American mental health professionals with master's degrees available for hiring. The agency is allowed by the State Department of Mental Health to use practitioners without master's degrees because of its rehabilitation model.

Since its inception, ACMHS has become well established in the Chinese community, developing a reputation for providing culturally sensitive services. This reputation is evidenced by the growth in its caseload, which consists of approximately five hundred people at any given time; a staff that works at maximum capacity; and a trend toward more clients referring themselves for treatment. Figure 12.1 shows the ACMHS's client breakdown by ethnicity between January and March 1997. During that period, the largest number of clients seen were Chinese (33 percent), followed by Vietnamese (19 percent) and Laotian (14 percent). These statistics are not surprising, given ACMHS's location.

Figure 12.1. Asian Community Mental Health Services Client Breakdown by Ethnicity.

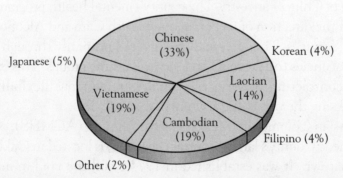

Source: Asian Community Mental Health Services, January–March 1997.

The large majority of the agency's clinical sessions are con-ducted in the clients' native language. Figure 12.2 shows the client breakdown by primary language between January and March 1997. The largest number of ACMHS clients speak Cantonese (21 per-cent), followed by Vietnamese (18 percent) and Cambodian (18 percent). Studies indicate that clients do well and remain in treat-ment with ethnicity and language matches (Flaskerud and Liu, 1991; Lin, 1994; Yeh, Takeuchi, and Sue, 1994).

The ACMHS clinical staff primarily serve the chronically men-tally ill. Figure 12.3 shows the client breakdown by diagnosis ac-cording to the *Diagnostic and Statistical Manual of Mental Disorders*, fourth edition, during the third quarter of 1997. The largest num-ber of clients (44 percent) suffered from mood disorders, followed by schizophrenia and other psychotic disorders (40 percent) and anxiety disorders (10 percent).

Contributing to ACHMS's effectiveness is the fact that in ad-dition to its mental health services, it provides a number of other programs to the community. Services are provided to nearly six hundred primarily monolingual Asians and Pacific Islanders with developmental disabilities. In conjunction with the Regional Cen-ter of the East Bay, clients are offered case management, parent

Figure 12.2. Asian Community Mental Health Services Client Breakdown by Primary Language.

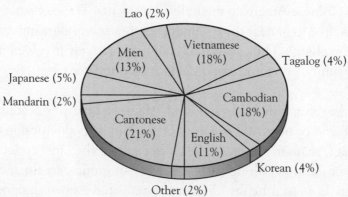

Source: Asian Community Mental Health Services, 1997.

Figure 12.3. Asian Community Mental Health Services Client Breakdown by Diagnosis.

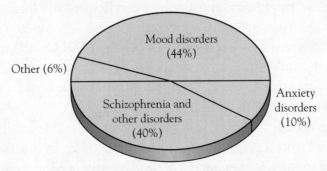

Note: Diagnosis is according to *Diagnostic and Statistical Manual of Mental Disorders,* fourth edition.
Source: Asian Community Mental Health Services, 1997.

training and support, resource development, and advocacy. ACHMS also serves as the lead agency for Asian Sisters in Action, a coalition of East Bay community agencies that address alcohol, tobacco, and other drug abuse among young Asian Pacific women. Finally, ACHMS has one program directed at high-risk youth, Prevention Services for At-Risk Youth, and another aimed at preventing substance abuse among youth, Regional Alliance for Community Empowerment.

Through the use of community-based multiservice organizations such as ACMHS, Alameda County appears to be meeting the needs of its Chinese American mentally ill residents. These organizations are located in or near the communities they serve, allowing easy access for clients. They also allow staff to be actively involved in the community, providing support, education, and consultation.

Los Angeles, San Francisco, and Alameda counties account for 4,460,758 or nearly 63 percent of the Chinese population in California (*Asians in America,* 1991). Because of the large concentration of Chinese, along with other Asian groups, in these areas, effective mental health delivery systems have been designed to meet their mental health needs. Unfortunately, in counties such as Riverside and San Bernardino, where relatively few Chinese reside (13,166 in both counties) and where they are dispersed over a large geographic area, no specialized, culturally sensitive mental health programs are available. Consequently, we can assume that mental health services are underutilized by Chinese immigrants living in these counties. The challenge for human service professionals is to advocate for culturally sensitive mental health delivery systems that reach out and serve Chinese living in rural areas or scattered among the general population.

Although their numbers are steadily growing, there is still a need for more master's-level bilingual and bicultural Chinese mental health professionals. There is also a need for culturally sensitive board and care facilities, residential treatment programs, and long-term care facilities, not only in California but in cities and counties throughout the United States. Finally, there is a need for bicultural therapeutic models that can be used effectively to improve the well-being of mentally ill Chinese clients and their families.

Services for Children and Adolescents

Government agencies and funding sources have traditionally been supportive of services to children, no matter what the political and economic climate. This is due, in part, to the belief that the problems of children are the result of circumstances beyond their control, the social ills of the time, or perhaps dysfunctional parents. Consequently, although funding for human services continues to dwindle, strong efforts are still being made to meet the welfare, social service, and mental health needs of children and adolescents.

Unfortunately, there is a rising trend of juvenile delinquency, gang involvement (with estimates of three thousand gang members in Los Angeles and thirty-two hundred in Orange County), and substance abuse among Asian American groups. Reports of child abuse and neglect are also increasing. Whether this is a reflection of an actual increase in child abuse or simply the result of better recognition and reporting is not clear. In any case, culturally sensitive programs and services are needed to serve abusive and neglectful parents and their children.

Juvenile Delinquency, Gang Involvement, and Substance Abuse

As with other groups, the increase in juvenile delinquency, gang involvement, and substance abuse among Chinese and other Asian American groups is due in great part to family dysfunction, poverty, and peer pressure. In 1988, to address the needs of delinquent adolescents and gang members, the Los Angeles County Probation Department established the Asian Gang Unit. The unit is now recognized by other law enforcement agencies, schools, social service providers, and the community for its expertise and effectiveness in working with Asian American youth and their families. In addition to working directly with gang members, the unit's members are called upon to share their knowledge at community meetings and criminal justice seminars. The unit has also established the Vision Mentoring Program, which is designed to offer alternatives to gang activities for teens who have been arrested for felonies and are on probation. The program is supported primarily by volunteers who are interested in helping troubled Asian youth. Unfortunately, the unit is the only one of its kind in California. In addition, it is understaffed, with six probation officers, only two of whom are Chinese, covering all of Los Angeles County. Few Asian Americans have been willing to enter this area of law enforcement.

In addition to law enforcement agencies, numerous private nonprofit agencies provide counseling to drug-dependent and troubled Chinese youth and their families. Besides counseling, the emphasis is on establishing and supporting community or school-based programs aimed at prevention and early-intervention services designed to resolve crises, prevent substance abuse, and divert problems from the legal system. The Asian Pacific Family Center in Rosemead, California, for example, has school-based services at nine local schools.

There is also an emphasis on more collaboration between child-focused agencies and organizations. An example of this is the Healthy Start Program, initiated by Governor Pete Wilson of California in 1992. The program awarded $400,000 to agencies over a four-year period to establish and operate a school-based resource center. Located and working together in the resource center are representatives from the contract agency and mental health, health services, juvenile justice, and social services. The objectives of the program are prevention, early intervention, and coordination of services related to substance abuse, juvenile delinquency, child abuse and neglect, mental health, and health-related problems.

The Chinatown Service Center (CSC) in Los Angeles was one of the first to be awarded a contract. Even though its four-year grant period has ended, CSC continues to support the Healthy Start Program, located on the grounds of Castelar Elementary School in Chinatown. It has been demonstrated to be effective, and there are now over one hundred such programs throughout California.

Child Abuse

Reaching out and serving the needs of Chinese American families in which child abuse or neglect has occurred is more difficult than serving those in need of mental health services. Unlike mental health, social service departments in California cannot contract essential services to community-based agencies such as emergency response, family investigation, court dependency, family maintenance, or family reunification, because of legal mandates. Consequently, child abuse and neglect services are centralized and therefore are not normally located in or near Chinese communities.

Recognizing this problem, the Asian Pacific Policy and Planning Council and the Asian Child Abuse Council worked for years with Los Angeles' Department of Children and Family Services (DCFS) to establish the Asian Pacific Project. The goal of the project is family preservation; it aims to improve the quality of services offered to the Asian Pacific population by providing immediate culturally and linguistically appropriate child welfare services to families in the Asian Pacific community. The objectives of the project are

1. To establish a full-service district for Asian Pacific bilingual and bicultural services for the community, including protective services and family prevention services

2. To provide vertical case management protective services to the Asian Pacific community, thereby improving continuity of service (having one instead of several workers providing the essential services as is normally the case)

3. To provide augmented specialized services to the community, including child abuse prevention, community education, and family preservation

4. To act in a community relations role and provide consultation to DCFS about the Asian Pacific community in an effort to improve services in areas such as staff training and foster care recruitment

5. To provide a setting for evaluating and researching methods of improving child welfare services to the Asian Pacific community in areas such as casework methods, service needs, assessment, and case identification

The project has proved to be very successful. At its inception, the unit opened with one Chinese-speaking social worker. At the end of 1991, the unit had ten such workers. Today, the unit consists of six supervising social workers and thirty-nine children's social workers. The unit's staff is centrally located; however, they spend practically all of their time in the field, either visiting their clients, consulting, networking, or providing community education.

Table 12.7 shows the Asian Pacific Project statistics on intakes for reports of suspected physical abuse, sexual abuse, or neglect from 1989 through 1996; the figures do not reflect the number of families that are still being seen. The number of intakes rose from 335 in 1989, of which 67 (20 percent) were Chinese, to 1,922 in 1996, of

Table 12.7. Asian Pacific Project Statistics on Intakes for Suspected Physical Abuse, Sexual Abuse, or Neglect, 1989–1996.

Year	Cambodian	Chinese	Filipino/ Japanese	Korean	Lao/ Thai	Samoan/ Tongan	Vietnamese	Total
1989	158	67	0	0	0	0	110	335
1990	546	298	0	74	0	0	318	1,236
1991	568	355	0	163	0	0	608	1,694
1992	511	306	23	223	84	9	539	1,695
1993	651	348	73	206	43	53	539	1,913
1994	559	414	99	230	89	41	508	1,940
1995	596	429	96	269	59	33	433	1,915
1996	514	466	111	253	104	40	434	1,922
Total	4,103	2,693	402	1,418	379	176	3,489	12,650

Source: Los Angeles County Department of Children and Family Services, *Asian Pacific Project Statistics on Intakes, 1989–1996.*

whom 466 (24 percent) were Chinese. In 1996, there were 466 intakes of Chinese suspected of physical abuse, sexual abuse, or neglect. Given that there are approximately 190,000 Chinese eighteen years of age and younger living in Los Angeles County (U.S. Bureau of the Census, 1990), the number of intakes indicates that approximately one in four hundred Chinese children are reported to have been abused or neglected. This figure is significantly lower than the ratio of one in four generally reported in California. Statistically this means that 0.25 per 100 Chinese are reported for suspected child abuse. This is low in comparison with the number for the general population, which is 7.10 per 100 (State of California, 1996). It is unknown whether this indicates that Chinese tend not to abuse or neglect their children or whether the cases of abuse are still undetected. Research in this area is needed to help answer this question.

Figure 12.4 compares the reasons for referral for suspected abuse of Asian American children in Los Angeles County in 1996 with those of the general population of the United States in 1994.

**Figure 12.4. Asian Pacific Project Comparison of the
Reasons for Suspected Child Abuse Between
Asian Americans in Los Angeles County in 1996
and the General Population in the United States in 1994.**

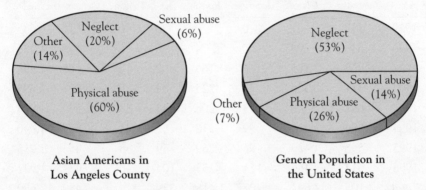

Asian Americans in
Los Angeles County

General Population in
the United States

Source: County of Los Angeles, Asian Pacific Project, 1996; U.S. Department of Health and Human Services, 1996.

Among Asian Americans, physical abuse, at 60 percent, was the most common reason for referrals being made, with neglect (20 percent), other reasons (14 percent), and sexual abuse (6 percent) less commonly seen. These figures are in marked contrast to the generally publicized statistics on the general population in the United States that indicate the most common reason for referrals to be suspected neglect (53 percent), followed by physical abuse (26 percent), other reasons (7 percent), and sexual abuse (14 percent). The low figures on suspected neglect among Asian Americans probably reflect the extent to which Asian parents use relatives to supervise their children, and the low reporting of sexual abuse may reflect the strong cultural attitude Asians have toward enforcing generational and sexual boundaries.

Table 12.8 shows the Asian Pacific Project's number of cases on hand by language in 1996. The largest number of cases for Chinese (279) were seen in June. This represented 23 percent of the 1,206 cases in the unit that month. The small number of Chinese cases in the unit lends evidence to the premise that Chinese parents are not

Table 12.8. Asian Pacific Project Cases on Hand Each Month by Language, 1996.

Language	Jan.	Feb.	Mar.	Apr.	May	June	July	Aug.	Sept.	Oct.	Nov.	Dec.
Cambodian	260	299	318	320	325	343	285	278	228	276	291	301
Vietnamese	249	261	289	262	278	280	262	242	228	260	288	243
Chinese	198	192	214	242	263	279	222	206	214	260	271	207
Korean	156	150	176	168	155	156	130	129	121	123	134	126
Tagalog	47	52	49	61	69	59	63	59	60	64	61	53
Japanese	30	28	31	33	35	38	43	44	60	61	54	29
Tongan/Samoan	25	27	27	30	32	30	27	22	25	30	27	27
Laotian/Thai	24	24	23	19	26	21	22	21	20	21	19	21
Total	989	1,033	1,127	1,135	1,183	1,206	1,054	1,001	956	1,095	1,145	1,007

Source: County of Los Angeles, Asian Pacific Project, 1996.

abusive. However, as indicated previously, research is needed to determine whether this is true or whether abuse in Chinese families is simply not being adequately detected and reported.

The number of out-of-home placements for Chinese and other abused or neglected Asian American children is relatively low. However, there are too few foster care placements to match the ethnicity of the children. In 1994, for example, the Asian Pacific Project had ninety-nine children in out-of-home placements. Of these children, twenty-four or 24 percent were placed with relatives, eight or 8 percent were placed in foster homes of the same ethnicity, forty or 40 percent were placed in foster homes of a different ethnicity, and twenty-seven or 27 percent were placed in group homes of a different ethnicity. In other words, sixty-seven children or 67 percent were in out-of-home placements where the caretakers were of a different ethnicity.

The social service and child welfare needs of Chinese youth and their families is on the rise, with a continuing increase in juvenile delinquency, gang involvement, substance abuse, and reporting of child abuse. Fortunately, government agencies and funding sources continue to make services to children and adolescents a high priority. Consequently, strong efforts still are being made to provide counseling, school-and community-based programs, and coordination of services among agencies to families that need these services.

The Los Angeles County Department of Children and Family Services took a progressive step toward meeting the child welfare needs of Chinese and other Asian American children by establishing the Asian Pacific Project. Regrettably, it is the only one of its kind in California and perhaps in the country. Other county social service departments have elected not to use the model and are providing services in the traditional manner. We can therefore only assume that the delivery of services to Chinese and other Asian groups in this critical area is not being adequately addressed.

In addition, there is a lack of bilingual and bicultural foster homes or homes with foster parents of the same ethnicity as the

Chinese children placed in them. The lack of same-ethnicity foster homes may exacerbate the separation problems of children in placement, who may become revictimized by being subjected to a strange and alien culture. A partial solution to this problem is to pay a small fee to Asian American foster parents to keep them available to receive children with the same ethnic identity.

Given the increasing number of child abuse cases being reported, there is a need for additional bilingual and bicultural Chinese American child welfare professionals. There is also a critical shortage of Chinese-speaking juvenile probation officers. It is hoped that graduate and undergraduate schools, including psychology and social work programs, will increase their efforts to recruit students to help fill these shortages.

On August 22, 1996, President Bill Clinton signed the Personal Responsibility and Work Opportunity Reconciliation Act of 1996 as part of welfare reform. The passage of this act will have a tremendous impact on our nation and on the lives of a great number of people and their families. Many of those who will be affected include legal immigrants and children. Although welfare reform was intended to prevent fraud in the system and misuse of government aid, one unfortunate consequence has been the adverse impact it has had on legitimate welfare cases and people who are genuinely in need, many of whom are Chinese. Among other things, the Act limits the length of time families can receive public assistance to two years. As a result, many families will be made to suffer poverty and humiliation when, through no fault of their own, they lose their welfare benefits. If sufficient social and vocational rehabilitation services are not provided to help these families, child and substance abuse, juvenile delinquency, gang involvement, and crime will increase.

Adult Services

The funding for adult services and programs to assist Chinese in the areas of substance abuse, domestic violence, immigration, and issues related to the elderly is limited and dwindling. Individuals and families who need such services are often at the brink of a crisis, abuse, poverty, or serious mental illness. Regrettably, as so often happens, those who need the most services receive the fewest.

Substance Abuse

Substance abuse is becoming a greater problem among Chinese Americans. Compared to the past, immigrants now account for a larger portion of Chinese drug and alcohol users. Unfortunately, only a few nonprofit agencies continue to serve them and other Asian groups, for example, the Asian American Drug Abuse Program (AADAPT) in Los Angeles and Asian American Recovery Services (AARS) in San Francisco. AADAPT was established in 1972 and AARS in 1985. Both have diverse funding sources; provide a full range of substance abuse services, including a residential treatment program; and are staffed by bilingual and bicultural professionals and paraprofessionals. They also target their programs toward both adults and children, have prevention and community-based programs, and serve a large geographic area. However, they continue to struggle to obtain the funds necessary for sustaining their programs.

Domestic Violence

Reporting of domestic violence among Chinese and other Asian groups is increasing; this is reflected in the culturally sensitive shelters now available for Asian American women and the growth in domestic violence groups for Asian American men. Largely through Asian women's advocacy groups and shelter organizations, Chinese and other Asian American women are now being educated regarding their rights and provided with services to address their special needs. The Center for the Pacific-Asian Family, for example, provides the following programs and services:

Programs

1. Domestic violence (shelter and nonshelter)
2. Sexual assault assistance
3. Child abuse treatment and prevention

Services

1. Telephone hot line counseling
2. Confidential emergency shelter (thirty to forty-five days)
3. Psychosocial assessment
4. Individual, group, and family counseling
5. Case management
6. Victim advocacy
7. Nonshelter services (counseling and legal assistance)
8. Information and referral
9. Counseling for adolescent victims of abuse
10. Counseling for child abuse victims or children exposed to domestic violence
11. Legal assistance

The Asian Women's Shelter, started by a group of ten women who volunteered for four years to help battered women, provides similar services in the San Francisco/Oakland area. However, there are only five such organizations in the country, with the others located in Los Angeles, New York City, Boston, and Chicago.

Immigrant Services

As the number of Chinese immigrants to this country continues to rise, they have a greater need for agencies to help them adapt to their new environment. One such organization is the Gum Moon

Women's Residence (GMWR) and Asian Women's Resource Center (AWRC), located in San Francisco's Chinatown. Among other services, this organization provides a transitional living program for women, tutoring, English as a Second Language programs, day care for children, and information and referral services. Unfortunately, the GMWR and AWRC is one of only a few community-based agencies whose major goal is to serve recent Chinese immigrants.

The Elderly

The needs of the Chinese elderly are well documented (Yu, 1986; Browne and Broderick, 1994; Mui, 1996). The number of Chinese elders, who are typically overlooked by policy makers and planners, is expected to increase dramatically by the next century. Already, the majority of Chinese American elderly are foreign-born. Their needs have been studied (Yu, 1986; Browne and Broderick, 1994; Mui, 1996), but services to meet them are very slow in coming. The elderly suffer from depression, health problems, and stresses associated with immigration, including language barriers, acculturation problems, poverty, social isolation, splitting of the household, and adjustment to newborn or new immigrant family members.

Some agencies, like the Chinatown Senior Service Center in Los Angeles, provide low-rent housing and a full range of services to the Chinese elderly. However, such centers are few and are generally located in areas that have a large concentration of Chinese. Compounding the problem is the fact that elderly foreign-born Chinese are much less likely than their Caucasian counterparts to be identified by service providers and are less likely to receive treatment (Chi and Boey, 1993).

The needs of Chinese adults in the areas of substance abuse, domestic violence, immigration, and the elderly are not adequately being met. Regrettably, only in the area of domestic violence is enough attention being drawn to the need for increased services and programs to serve these high-risk groups.

Appendix A

Chinese Population in California by Counties

County	Population	Percentage
Los Angeles	245,033	35
San Francisco	127,140	18
Alameda	68,585	10
Santa Clara	65,027	9
Orange	41,403	6
San Mateo	32,487	4
Sacramento	25,125	4
Contra Costa	22,106	3
San Diego	19,686	3
San Bernardino	8,462	1
Other	49,796	7
Total	704,850	100

Source: "Asians in America," 1991, pp. 41, 44, 48.

Racial Population Groups of
Los Angeles County, 1990

Race	Population	Percentage
Caucasian	5,035,103	56.81
African American	992,974	11.20
Native American, Eskimo/Aleut	45,508	0.52
Native American	43,899	0.50
Eskimo	640	0.01
Aleut	969	0.01
Asian or Pacific Islander	954,485	10.77
Asian:		
Chinese	245,033	2.76
Filipino	219,653	2.48
Japanese	129,736	1.46
Asian Indian	43,829	0.49
Korean	145,431	1.64
Vietnamese	62,594	0.71
Cambodian	27,819	0.31
Hmong	359	0.00
Laotian	3,742	0.04
Thai	19,016	0.21
Other Asian	28,349	0.32
Pacific Islander:		
Hawaiian	8,009	0.09
Samoan	11,934	0.13
Tongan	1,546	0.02

Other Polynesian	537	0.01
Guamanian	5,632	0.06
Other Micronesian	201	0.00
Melanesian	578	0.01
Pacific Islander, not specified	487	0.01
Other Races	1,835,094	20.70
Male	4,421,398	49.89
Female	4,441,766	50.11
Total	8,863,164	100.00

Note: These figures do not count people of Hispanic origin as a separate category. People of Hispanic origin can be of any race.
Source: "Asians in America," 1991, p. 49.

Appendix C

Racial Population Groups
of San Francisco, 1990

Race	Population	Percentage
Caucasian	387,783	53.56
African American	79,039	10.92
Native American, Eskimo/Aleut	3,456	0.48
Native American	3,253	0.45
Eskimo	74	0.01
Aleut	129	0.02
Asian or Pacific Islander	210,876	29.13
Asian:		
Chinese	127,140	17.56
Filipino	42,652	5.89
Japanese	12,047	1.66
Asian Indian	3,063	0.42
Korean	6,240	0.86
Vietnamese	9,712	1.34
Cambodian	1,490	0.21
Hmong	4	0.00
Laotian	844	0.12
Thai	749	0.10
Other Asian	3,214	0.44
Pacific Islander:		
Hawaiian	957	0.13
Samoan	1,963	0.27
Tongan	141	0.02

Other Polynesian	40	0.01
Guamanian	420	0.06
Other Micronesian	31	0.00
Melanesian	95	0.01
Pacific Islander, not specified	74	0.01
Other Races	42,805	5.91
Male	362,497	50.07
Female	361,462	49.93
Total	723,959	100.00

Note: These figures do not count people of Hispanic origin as a separate category. People of Hispanic origin can be of any race.
Source: "Asians in America," 1991, p. 45.

Appendix D

Racial Population Groups of Alameda County, 1990

Race	Population	Percentage
Caucasian	761,815	59.55
African American	229,249	17.92
Native American, Eskimo/Aleut	8,894	0.70
Native American	8,532	0.67
Eskimo	162	0.01
Aleut	200	0.02
Asian or Pacific Islander	192,554	15.05
Asian:		
Chinese	68,585	5.36
Filipino	52,535	4.11
Japanese	13,592	1.06
Asian Indian	15,282	1.19
Korean	9,537	0.75
Vietnamese	13,374	1.05
Cambodian	3,538	0.28
Hmong	10	0.00
Laotian	2,895	0.23
Thai	791	0.06
Other Asian	4,420	0.35
Pacific Islander:		
Hawaiian	2,810	0.22
Samoan	1,143	0.09
Tongan	712	0.06

Other Polynesian	152	0.01
Guamanian	1,895	0.15
Other Micronesian	118	0.15
Melanesian	940	0.07
Pacific Islander, not specified	225	0.02
Other Races	86,670	6.78
Male	630,342	49.28
Female	648,840	50.72
Total	1,279,182	100.00

Note: These figures do not count people of Hispanic origin as a separate category. People of Hispanic origin can be of any race.
Source: "Asians in America," 1991, p. 42.

Appendix E

Immigration of Asian Groups, 1820–1994

Period	Chinese	Japanese	Asian Indian	Korean	Filipino	Vietnamese
1820	1	—	1	—	—	—
1821–1830	2	—	8	—	—	—
1831–1840	8	—	39	—	—	—
1841–1850	35	—	36	—	—	—
1851–1860	41,397	—	43	—	—	—
1861–1870	64,301	186	69	—	—	—
1871–1880	123,201	149	163	—	—	—
1881–1890	61,711	2,270	269	—	—	—
1891–1900	14,799	25,942	68	—	—	—
1901–1910	20,605	129,797	4,713	7,697	—	—
1911–1920	21,278	83,837	2,082	1,049	869	—
1921–1930	29,907	33,462	1,886	598	54,747	—
1931–1940	4,928	1,948	496	60	6,159	—
1941–1950	16,709	1,555	1,761	—	4,691	—
1951–1960	25,201	46,250	1,973	6,231	19,307	—
1961–1970	109,771	39,988	27,189	34,536	98,376	3,788
1971–1980	237,793	49,775	164,134	271,956	360,216	179,681
1981–1990[a]	446,000	44,800	261,900	338,800	495,300	401,400
1991–1994	282,900	28,995	154,587	79,435	239,465	233,992

[a]Figures for 1981–1990 are rounded to the nearest hundred.
Source: Adapted from Hing and Lee, 1996, p. 88.

Appendix F

Populations of Chinese in the United States by State, 1990

State	Chinese
Alabama	3,929
Alaska	1,342
Arizona	14,136
Arkansas	1,726
California	704,850
Colorado	8,695
Connecticut	11,082
Delaware	2,301
District of Columbia	3,144
Florida	30,737
Georgia	12,657
Hawaii	68,804
Idaho	1,420
Illinois	49,936
Indiana	7,371
Iowa	4,442
Kansas	5,330
Kentucky	2,736
Louisiana	5,430
Maine	1,262
Maryland	30,868
Massachusetts	53,792
Michigan	19,145

Minnesota	8,980
Mississippi	2,518
Missouri	8,614
Montana	655
Nebraska	1,775
Nevada	6,618
New Hampshire	2,314
New Jersey	59,084
New Mexico	2,607
New York	284,144
North Carolina	8,859
North Dakota	557
Ohio	19,447
Oklahoma	5,139
Oregon	13,652
Pennsylvania	29,562
Rhode Island	3,170
South Carolina	3,039
South Dakota	385
Tennessee	5,653
Texas	63,232
Utah	5,322
Vermont	679
Virginia	21,238
Washington	33,962
West Virginia	1,170
Wisconsin	7,354
Wyoming	554

Source: "Asians in America," 1991, p. 7.

Appendix G

Occupational Attainment of
Chinese Americans

Occupational Category	Native-Born (percent)	Immigrant (percent)
Professional	23	19
Executive/management	16	13
Technical/sales	40	31
Craft	6	6
Service	9	19
Equipment operator/laborer	6	12
Total	100	100

Note: Data are based on people throughout the United States sixteen years of age and older who last worked in 1985 or later.
Source: Adapted from Hing and Lee, 1996, p. 53.

Appendix H

Percentage of Families with Three or More Workers in 1989 Among Selected Asian and Pacific Islander Groups by Nativity and U.S. Citizenship

Families with Three or More Workers	All People (percent)	Native-Born (percent)	Total Foreign-Born (percent)	Total Naturalized Foreign-Born (percent)	Total Foreign-Born Noncitizens (percent)
General	13.3	12.8	18.5	18.5	18.6
Asian or Pacific Islander	19.8	18.0	20.2	24.2	16.1
Chinese American	19.0	14.4	19.9	21.4	18.0
Filipino American	29.6	21.8	31.1	32.9	26.8
Japanese American	15.2	18.7	6.8	14.5	4.9
Asian Indian American	17.6	12.3	17.9	21.0	15.2
Korean American	15.8	13.9	16.0	18.1	14.3
Vietnamese American	21.3	16.7	21.4	25.0	17.2
Cambodian American	13.5	15.2	13.5	25.1	10.3
Hmong American	6.75	8.3	6.7	16.8	5.2
Laotian American	18.9	13.1	18.9	30.3	15.8
Thai American	15.5	3.4	15.7	17.0	15.0
Pakistani American	15.0	20.35	15.0	17.5	12.5
Pacific Islander	19.7	19.9	19.4	20.6	18.4

Source: Adapted from Hing and Lee, 1996, p. 110.

References

Aponte, J., and VanDeusen, J. M. "Structural Family Therapy." In A. S. Gurman and D. P. Kniskern (eds.), *The Handbook of Family Therapy*. New York: Brunner/Mazel, 1981.

"Asians in America: 1990 Census." *Asian Week*, Aug. 1991.

Bandura, A. *Social Learning Theory*. Englewood Cliffs, N.J.: Prentice Hall, 1977.

Baucom, D. H., and Epstein, N. *Cognitive-Behavioral Marital Therapy*. New York: Brunner/Mazel, 1990.

Beck, A. T., Rush, A. J., Shaw, B. F., and Emery, G. *Cognitive Therapy of Depression*. New York: Guilford Press, 1979.

Beck, D. F., and Jones, M. A. *Progress on Family Problems*. New York: Family Service Association of America, 1973.

Boszormenyi-Nagy, I., and Spark, G. M. *Indivisible Loyalties*. New York Harper and Row, 1973.

Boszormenyi-Nagy, I., and Ulrich, D. N. "Contextual Family Therapy." In A. L. Gurman and D. P. Kniskern (eds.), *Handbook of Family Therapy*. New York: Brunner/Mazel, 1981.

Browne, C., and Broderick, A. "Asian and Pacific Island Elders: Issues for Social Work Practice and Education." *Social Work*, 1994, 39(3), 252–261.

California State Census Data Center. *State Census Data Source, 1990*. Sacramento: California State Census Data Center, 1990.

"California's 1996 Children's Justice Act Task Force Report." Sacramento: State of California, Office of Criminal Justice Planning, 1996.

Ch'en, K. *Buddhism in China*. Princeton, N.J.: Princeton University Press, 1973.

Chi, I., and Boey, K. W. *A Mental Health and Social Support Study of the Old-Old in Hong Kong*. Resource Paper Series no. 22. Hong Kong: University of Hong Kong, Department of Social Work and Social Administration, 1993.

Eberhard, W. *A History of China*. Berkeley: University of California Press, 1971.

Ellis, A., and others. *Rational-Emotive Couples Therapy*. New York: Pergamon Press, 1989.

English, J., and Feng, G. (trans.). *Lao Tsu: Tao Te Ching*. New York: Vantage Books, 1972.

Flaskerhud, J. H., and Liu, P. Y. "Effects of an Asian Client-Therapist Language, Ethnicity, and Gender Match on Utilization and Outcome of Therapy." *Community Mental Health Journal*, 1991, *27*(1), 31–42.

Fong, R., and Mokuau, N. "Not Simply 'Asian Americans': Periodical Literature Review on Asian and Pacific Islanders." *Social Work*, 1994, *39*(3), 298–306.

Freeman, J. M. *Changing Identities: Vietnamese Americans, 1975–1995*. Boston: Allyn and Bacon, 1995.

Gibson, C. M. "Empowerment Theory and Practice with Adolescents of Color in the Child Welfare System." *Families in Society*, 1993, *7*(7), 387–396.

Haley, J. *Problem-Solving Therapy*. (2nd ed.) San Francisco: Jossey-Bass, 1987.

Hartman, A., and Laird, J. *Family-Centered Social Work Practice*. New York: Free Press, 1983.

Hill, R. "Generic Features of Families Under Stress." In H. J. Parad (ed.), *Crisis Intervention: Selected Readings*. New York: Family Service Association of America, 1965.

Hing, H. O., and Lee, R. (eds.). *Reframing the Immigration Debate*. Los Angeles: LEAP Asian Pacific American Public Policy Institute and UCLA Asian American Studies Center, 1996.

Hsu, F.L.K. *Under the Ancestors' Shadow: Kinship, Personality and Social Mobility in China*. Stanford, Calif.: Stanford University Press, 1971.

Lee, E. "A Social Systems Approach to Assessment and Treatment for Chinese American Families." in M. McGoldrick, J. K. Pearce, and J. Giordano (eds.), *Ethnicity and Family Therapy*. New York: Guilford Press, 1982.

Libassi, M. F. "The Chronically Mentally Ill: A Practice Approach." In S. M. Rose (ed.), *Case Management and Social Work Practice*. White Plains, N.Y.: Longman, 1992.

Lin, L.C.H. "How Long Do Chinese Americans Stay in Psychotherapy?" *Journal of Counseling Psychology*, 1994, *41*(3), 288–291.

Loo, C., Tong, B., and True, R. "A Bitter Bean: Mental Health Status and Attitudes in Chinatown." *Journal of Community Psychology*, 1989, *17*, 283–296.

"Los Angeles County Cultural Competency Needs Assessment." Los Angeles: Los Angeles County Department of Mental Health, Program Support Bureau, Planning and Management Information Systems, 1997.

Lum, R. "Mental Health Attitudes and Opinions of Chinese." In J. Jones and C. Korchin (eds.), *Minority Mental Health*. New York: Praeger, 1982.

McGoldrick, M. "Ethnicity and Family Therapy: An Overview." In M. McGoldrick, J. K. Pearce, and J. Giordano (eds.), *Ethnicity and Family Therapy*. New York: Guilford Press, 1982.

Miller, J. G. "The Nature of Living Systems." *Behavioral Science*, 1975, *20*, 343–365.

Minuchin, S. *Families and Family Therapy*. Cambridge, Mass.: Harvard University Press, 1974.

Minuchin, S., and others. *Families of the Slums: An Exploration of Their Structure and Treatment*. New York: Basic Books, 1967.

Moxley, D. P. *The Practice of Case Management*. Thousand Oaks, Calif.: Sage, 1989.

Mui, A. "Depression Among Elderly Chinese: An Exploratory Study." *Social Work*, 1996, 41(6), 633–646.

Parad, H. J., and Parad, L. J. "A Study of Crisis-Oriented Planned Short-Term Treatment, Parts I and II." *Social Casework*, 1968, 49, 346–355.

Reid, W. J., and Epstein, L. *Task-Centered Casework*. New York: Columbia University Press, 1972.

Reischauer, E. O., and Fairbank, J. K. *East Asia: The Great Tradition*. Boston: Houghton Mifflin, 1960.

Robinson, R. H., and Johnson, W. L. *The Buddhist Religion: A Historical Introduction*. (3rd ed.) Belmont, Calif.: Wadsworth, 1982.

Rotter, J. B. *Social Learning and Clinical Psychology*. Englewood Cliffs. N.J.: Prentice Hall, 1954.

Rubin, A. "Case Management." In S. M. Rose (ed.), *Case Management and Social Work Practice*. White Plains, N.Y.: Longman, 1992.

Sue, S., and Sue, D. W. "Chinese-American Personality and Mental Health." In S. Sue and N. N. Wagner (eds.), *Asian Americans: Psychological Perspectives*. Palo Alto, Calif.: Science and Behavior Books, 1973.

Sung, B. L. *Mountains of Gold*. New York: Macmillan, 1967.

Tseng, G. W., and Hsu, J. *Culture and Family*. New York: Haworth Press, 1991.

Uba, L., and Sue, S. "Nature and Scope of Services for Asian and Pacific Islander Americans." In N. Mokuau (ed.), *Handbook of Social Services for Asian and Pacific Islanders*. Westport, Conn.: Greenwood Press, 1991.

U.S. Bureau of the Census. *Statistical Abstract of the United States*. Washington, D.C.: GPO, 1990.

U.S. Bureau of the Census. *Statistical Yearbook of the Immigration and Naturalization Service, 1990–1995*. Washington, D.C.: GPO, 1995.

U.S. Department of Health and Human Services, National Center on Child Abuse and Neglect. "Child Maltreatment 1994: Reports from the States to the National Center on Child Abuse and Neglect." Washington, D.C.: U.S. Government Printing Office, 1996.

Verny, T. R. "Analysis of Attrition Rates in a Psychiatric Outpatient Clinic." *Psychiatric Quarterly*. 1970, 44, 37–48.

Von Bertalanffy, L. *General Systems Theory*. New York: Braziller, 1968.

Waley, A. *The Analects of Confucius*. New York: Vintage Books, 1938.

Welch, H. *Taoism: The Parting of the Way*. Boston: Beacon Press, 1965.

Wells, R. A. *Planned Short-Term Treatment*. New York: Free Press, 1982.

Wessler, R. A., and Wessler, R. L. *The Principles and Practice of Rational-Emotive Therapy*. San Francisco: Jossey-Bass, 1980.

Williams, C.A.S. *Outlines of Chinese Symbolism and Art Motifs*. New York: Dover, 1976.

Yang, C. K. *Religion in Chinese Society*. Berkeley: University of California Press, 1961.

Yeh, M., Takeuchi, D. T., and Sue, S. "Asian-American Children Treated in the Mental Health System: A Comparison of Parallel and Mainstream Outpatient Service Centers." *Journal of Clinical Child Psychology*, 1994, *23*(1), 5–12.

Yu, E.S.H. "Health of the Chinese Elderly in America." *Research on Aging*, 1986, *8*(1), 84–109.

The Author

Marshall Jung is an associate professor in the Graduate Department of Social Work, California State University, San Bernardino. He also has a private practice and provides marital retreats and professional training at his retreat center in Lake Arrowhead, California. He received his M.S.W. degree (1971) from the University of Southern California and his D.S.W. degree (1974) from the University of Pennsylvania.

Jung has provided workshops and training programs for numerous family and social service agencies, veterans' and state hospitals, and mental health and child welfare organizations, as well as residential treatment facilities throughout the United States. He has provided workshops at the American Association of Marital and Family Therapy National Conference, the California Association of Marital and Family Therapists, the National Association of Social Workers National Conference, the California Chapter of the National Association of Social Workers, and the Family Service Association of America National Conference. He has also provided training in Hong Kong and Canada.

Jung is the author of *Constructual Marital Therapy: Theory and Practice* (1993) and *Romancing the Net*, with Richard Booth (1996). He has published papers in several major professional journals.

Index

utilization of, 207–209. *See also* Social services and resources

Mental illness: in case study, 185–194; Chinese attitudes toward, 4–5, 44–47, 186–187, 189–190, 194; ethnicity and, 44; psychosomatic symptoms and, 46–47. *See also* Chronic mental illness

Mental Research Institute, 103

Mental Retardation Facilities and Community Mental Centers Construction Act of 1963, 196–197, 206–207

Mental status evaluation, 188

Metalevel communication, 96, 116, 192

Metropolitan State Hospital, 213

Miller, J. G., 59

Minuchin, S., 24, 89, 90, 93

Miracle question, 105, 106

Model minorities, 2, 32–33, 197–198

Modeling of therapist: of marital interaction, 160; of parent-child interaction, 125, 134; of reflective listening skills, 160, 171–172

Mokuau, N., 32

Moral principles: in Buddhism, 40; in Confucianism, 37

Morales, R., 196

Moxley, D. P., 61

Mui, A., 230

Murase, K., 196

Mysticism, Taoist, 39

N

National Child Welfare Grant, 197

National Institute of Mental Health, 196, 197, 215

Negative circular communication, 93–95

Negative reciprocal interactions, 68, 69

Neutrality, therapist, 85; in case examples, 120, 170

New Jersey, Chinese-American concentration in, 200, 201, 242

New York, Chinese-American concentration in, 201, 242

Nishinaka, G., 196

Nonaction, 38–39

Normalizing of feelings, 65–66, 120; in depression case study, 148; in intergenerational conflict case study, 181

O

Oakland, Asian Community Mental Health Services in, 201, 215–218. *See also* Alameda County

Obedience, 49

Occupational attainment, of Chinese Americans, 243

Okura, P., 196

Operant conditioning, 67–68

Overgeneralization, 102

P

Pacific Clinics, 211–212

Pacific Islanders, 32, 33, 245

Pakistini Americans, 245

Paper son, 10–11

Parad, H. J., 96

Parad, L. J., 96

Paradoxical situation, 133

Parental authority: and parentified children, 77; therapist support for, 82–83. *See also* Hierarchical relationships

Parent-child conflict: in depression case study, 143–153; in Lee family case study, 115–126, 127–141. *See also* Intergenerational conflict

Parentification of children, 76–77, 90, 109; in chronic mental illness case study, 190, 192–193; interventions for, 192–193

Parents: building on positive intentions of, 124, 126, 135; modeling for, 125, 134; need for approval of, in case study, 143–153; unwillingness of, to compromise, 79–80

Pasadena Child Guidance Clinic, 211

Peck, S., 45

Peller, J. E., 103

Perceptions, 99

Personal Responsibility and Work Opportunity Reconciliation Act of 1996, 227

Personalization, 102

Philadelphia Child Guidance Clinic, 89, 93

Planned Short-Term Treatment, 5, 96–98, 110–111; treatment implications of, 98

Planned Short-Term Treatment (Wells), 96

Polygamy, 26

Polytheism, 35–36

Pop psychology, 45–46

Positive, emphasizing the, 103–104; exception question for, 146; in initial interview, 118. *See also* Solution Focused Therapy

Positive reciprocal interactions, 68–69

Positive treatment atmosphere, 81–82